"I DO"

To Marry or Not to Marry, that's the Question!

H. NIGEL KASSEMBE

THIS BOOK IS DEDICATED TO:

My wife TJ: for being such a wonderful wife, we have come a long way, 23 years of marriage and we are still going strong. I look forward to growing old together, love you always!

My children: Imani, Nigel, and (RIP Isaiah), for being such great kids, I have enjoyed parenting and watching you guys grow up to be such mature and wonderful people, keep up the good work, love you guys always!

CONTENTS

INTRODUCTION

Marriage is a very wonderful institution if it is working, but if it is not working, it can be a very awful institution. Am I right or wrong? I think I'm right! Because I mean, how awful would it be to be stuck in a bad relationship because you are not supposed to call it quits just like that. You know, to be stuck in a relationship that is awful but you can't just tell the other person that you don't want to be with them anymore without having to not only deal with going through a divorce situation (which can turn out to be very ugly, involving the court system and all that), but also having to deal with the feeling of being a failure in marriage, not only in the eyes of your family and friends, but also in the eyes of God as well, because you did swear till death do us part, so help me God, didn't you? So as you can see, there can be a lot of pressures for people to stay in their marriages even if it doesn't seem to be working, because not only have they vowed to be with their partners for life in the eyes of their family and friends, but they have also (most often) vowed in the eyes of God as well, and who wants to disappoint God, not me, do you, I don't think so! And so this is how people can find themselves in an awful marriage but find it very hard to breakaway and end their awful marriage, and it's because there can be a lot of pressure for them to stay and to keep trying to make it work somehow, until the marriage starts to become very unhealthy and or toxic for one or both partners, leaving them with no choice but to divorce.

And this is why a lot of people are scared of marriage, and it's because no one wants to be stuck in a marriage that sucks, you know what I mean? But there are millions and millions of people out there who are in marriages that suck and they don't know how to either get out of them or how to go about fixing them and try to make them better. I mean it's crazy how millions and millions of people each year vow to love and cherish each other on their wedding day only to end up hating and not caring for each other just a few short years after they are married. I mean it's crazy, but a marriage can turn ugly in a very short period of time, if the couple doesn't learn how to be married to each other. And notice how I said "learn how to be married to each other", and what I mean by this is that, the couple hasn't learned how to operate in the relationship with each other in an orderly way that is acceptable to each other in order to make the marriage relationship run in a more smoothly manner, you know, the couple learns how to work together to make the marriage a more enjoyable and or a less stressful unit. But it takes both partners to want to work at their marriage for the marriage to actually have a realistic chance of becoming a good marriage and lasting forever.

And so, yes, the institution of marriage can be an awful institution if it is not working, but if it is working, it can be a very wonderful institution. Because think about it, how wonderful would it be to find the person who ends up not only being the love of your life, but the two of you actually end up enjoying the bliss of being married to each other for a very long time, you know, the two of you end up being joyfully married to each other till the both of you are old and gray. I mean, how wonderful would that be? I think that would be so excellently wonderful, don't you? And that is the hope of marriage, isn't it? Isn't the hope is to marry someone that you truly love and someone who truly loves you and the two of you live happily ever after? I think that is all of our hopes and wishes, right? And that is why when we say our vows on our wedding day we don't say "I will try", no, we say "I Do", meaning you won't just try, you will go beyond trying, you will do it, meaning you will do whatever you have to do to make the marriage relationship work, you know, so the marriage relationship can be not only a long lasting one, but so that the marriage relationship can also be a more enjoyable one. And this is when the institution of marriage is a wonderful one, and it's when the couple learns how to actually operate in it with love for one another, you know, when the couple knows how to deal with each other in a manner that is complementary and or uplifting to each other. And this is what marriage is supposed to be all about, it is supposed to be about two people joining their lives together and spending the rest of their lives caring and uplifting each other as husband and wife. But as we all know, a lot of couples just don't seem to be able to learn how to operate as a unit, you know, a lot of couples just don't learn how to care and uplift each other, a lot of couples just don't learn how to be married to each other, and therefore they end up finding themselves in a marriage that is not working.

Marriage is not an easy institution, it demands a lot of commitment, discipline, and proper communication. And notice how I said "proper communication", and what I mean by proper is, the partners should know how to speak to each other in a manner that allows for conversation to be able to flow back and forth between the couple with ease and without any malice and or any spitefulness. And what I mean is, the couple should be able to speak to each other in a manner that brings understanding rather than in a manner that can cause more confusion in the marriage, you know, like if one partner has a habit of blaming and or diminishing the other partner, or yelling and shouting at the other partner, or being rude and dismissive of the other partner, all these are examples of bad communication between the couple, which will do nothing but bring misery and frustration into the marriage, which will cause the marriage to suffer and most likely come to an end sooner than later. So good communication is perhaps the most important key in determining whether a couple will have a good marriage or not, because good communication brings about good understanding, and good understanding brings about less confusion in the marriage, and less confusion will bring about more joy in the marriage, as the couple will have a good understanding of each other, which will allow them to be able to run their marriage more smoothly as a unit.

Marriage is a gamble, as no one truly knows if their marriage will be long lasting or not, as there's no way of telling if the marriage will be able to stand the test of time. But, there are some things that we can do to increase our chances of ending up with a long lasting marriage. One of the most crucial things that we can do to increase our odds of having a long lasting marriage is finding and or picking the right person to marry. Picking the right person to marry is perhaps the most crucial thing we can do to increase our chances of having a long lasting marriage, because that person will most likely want to fight to make the marriage work, unlike if we marry the wrong person, who will most likely do nothing but use us and misuse us and then run and hide at the first signs of marital challenges. So how do we go about finding and or picking the right person to marry anyway? Well, we'll talk about it in the second chapter of the book called: Finding Mr. or Mrs. Right.

The other most crucial thing that we can do to increase our chances of having a long lasting marriage is to learn how to be married to our spouse. You see, marriage is not a science, no, it's an art form, and no art is exactly the same, which means no marriage is exactly like another marriage, which means you can't just copy how another couple operate their marriage for success, no, you have to develop your own operating method in your marriage that works for you and your partner, because the two of you are different people from another couple, and so what works for them may not actually work for you. And I mean, sure you can borrow a little method here and there from a different couple and see if it will work for you and your partner, but you can't rely on just borrowing, no, you and your partner will actually have to discover the unique qualities about each other and develop a way of doing things between the two of you that will be acceptable to the both of you. You see, like I said, marriage is not a science, no, it's an art form. So, how do we go about learning how to be married to our spouses anyway? Well, we'll talk about that in chapter 5 of the book called: The Honeymoon is Over.

Picking the right person to marry and learning how to be married to that person are really the two most crucial things that we can do in order to increase our chances in having a long lasting marriage. A marriage truly hinges on these two things and or on these two factors. Let's get into the book and talk more about marriage and see what we can discover about how we can go about increasing our chances of having a long lasting happy marriage. Did you notice how I said "happy marriage", not just long lasting. And the reason why I said "happy" marriage is because there's really no point in having a long lasting marriage if the marriage is not a happy one, you know what I mean? I mean, I don't know about you, but I for sure wouldn't want to be in a long lasting marriage if the marriage is not a happy one, I don't think you would either. Now, of course not everyday will be all happy happy, but the marriage should not be all gloomy and or miserable all the time, or the majority of the time, no, there should be more joyful days than gloomy days. And as time goes on in the marriage, the gloomy days should be so few that the couple can't even remember them. And that's what a happy marriage is, it's a marriage where the couple can't even remember the last time they had a fight, or the last time they were too mad to talk to each other, or the last time they didn't want to be next to each other. When your marriage gets to where arguments become too small for either one of you to be fazed and or even remember them, then most likely than not you and your spouse have a happy marriage, because you will have learnt how to deal with the small stuff before they become big issues.

Anyway, let's get into the book, because I think I have learned a lot about marriage having been married for 23 years now (and still going strong) to my lovely wife, and so I think I may have some good wisdom to share about marriage that whoever reads this book may enjoy and gain some wisdom from it. Before I got married (when I was in my single days) I never really thought I had what it took to be in a marriage, you know, I really didn't think I had what it takes to be able to maintain a long lasting marriage. And this is because I just didn't think I had the patience that a marriage really requires. But over the years I learned how to be patient and I learned how to be married, especially how to be married to my wife. So now, 23 years later, as I look back into our marriage, I am amazed at how we have been able to navigate through the tests that had come our way and how we have been able to learn how to be married to each other despite the few major obstacles and or differences that really challenged our marriage in the early years of our marriage. And so, looking back, I have learned a lot about what it really takes to increase the chance of having a long lasting happy marriage, and I think it's time I share some of what I have learnt, as any true writer would. Oh, my writing style is kinda crazy and I tend to be all over the place from time to time, but I usually get back on topic, so don't worry, I won't lose you too much, lol.

Thank you for taking time to read this book, I hope you will enjoy it, and please feel free to give me any feedback (IDothebook@gmail.com) on what you think about the book, and whether you agreed or disagreed with anything I said and or with any advice that I gave. Thanks again, and let's get into the book!

"I DO"

1

JOURNEY TO LOVE

Wow, I can't believe I've actually been married for 23 years now and still going strong with my lovely wife. It seems like it was just yesterday that we said "I Do" to each other down at the courthouse in D.C. in front of a judge. I remember looking outside the window at the street where I used to ride my bike as a teenager (our apartment building was on the same street that ran down all the way to the courthouse building). I remember standing there (as the judge started the ceremony) looking outside the window (which was right behind where my soon to be wife was standing) and thinking to myself "wow, I'm actually about to do this, I'm actually about to get married". I could feel fear and trepidation start to overcome me, but then I switched my eyes from the window and focused on my lovely soon to be wife and my fear and trepidation went away and I joyfully said "I Do". Then the judge pronounced us husband and wife and I proceeded to kiss my wife and then we left the courthouse as a newly married couple.

The whole ceremony did not take more than ten minutes, and I don't think we were at the courthouse for more than one hour (including checking in and waiting almost half an hour for the judge to come to the ceremony room (the judge was running late that day, apparently it was a busier than usual Thursday for civil weddings). Actually, we too were running late, my wife was having her hair done that morning and it was taking longer than it was supposed to and I was getting very nervous that we were gonna miss our scheduled wedding time. So when she finally got home from getting her hair done, we threw on our clothes and ran to the car and sped off to downtown D.C. When we got to the courthouse we hurried to the ceremony room and was glad that the judge was not ready yet. The ceremony was nice and short, and we only had a few people to witness our special day (a few family members who could make it). It actually felt like we were eloping, lol, as none of our parents were there, for various reasons (I will explain a little bit more in another chapter). But that was a nice, short and sweet ceremony, and very inexpensive, lol.

Oh, we also did not have a reception or go on our honeymoon, lol, oops, my bad, I didn't plan things well, hey I was super young (okay, I was not that young, unless 24 yrs old is super young), but my wife keeps reminding me every once in while that I owe her a reception and a honeymoon. So I guess even after 23 years of marriage a reception and a honeymoon is still needed, okay fine, I'm about to plan the most romantic getaway honeymoon ever, and I will plan the most extravagant wedding reception ever (if this book makes the best sellers list, lol), and all who happen to read this book will be invited to witness a most majestic wedding ceremony to make up for the ceremony I owe my wife from 23 years ago. But, if Covid 19 is still around, I guess my wife is just gonna have to wait just a little bit longer, just a little bit, hey, this time it's not my fault, there's Coronavirus out there people, lol.

Anyway, yeah, 23 years of marriage and still going strong is very amazing, especially for me. And the reason why I say "especially for me" is because I never really thought of myself as being the marriage type, before I got married. And what I mean by "marriage type" is, I never thought I had what it took to maintain a marriage. And what I mean by "to maintain a marriage" is, I never thought I had what it took to make a marriage work, you know, I never thought I had the patience, commitment, perseverance, discipline, etc., that is required to be able to have and maintain a long term relationship. I mean truth be told, before I got married I was scared of relationships. And the reason why I was scared of relationships is because, for one, I could tell relationships required a lot of energy, sacrifice and commitment, and for a person like me who enjoyed their independence (you know, to do whatever I wanted without anyone to answer to), and a person like me who had a lot of dreams and ambitions (like: basketball, music career, writing books, making movies), I did not see how I could actually be in a serious relationship and still pursue all of my dreams and aspirations. I reasoned it would be impossible, just not enough time and energy to do both, one or two of those things would suffer, you know, either my dreams and aspirations would suffer or my relationship would suffer. So I really didn't think settling down and being married was in the cards for me, because my dreams and aspirations were too big and too many for me to even imagine that I would have the time and energy to actually nurture a marriage, knowing how much work and commitment a marriage requires.

The second reason why I didn't think that I could handle a serious relationship and actually maintain it is because, I just didn't think I had the patience to deal with the various nuances that are part of relationships, you know, emotions, moods, arguments, disagreements, misunderstandings, miscommunication, not being on the same page, etc, in that manner. You see, the way I grew up I had to brush a lot of emotions off my shoulders and keep it moving, you know, no room for expressing feelings (how you feeling, if anything is bothering you inside) or anything like that, no, you toughen yourself up emotionally and you keep it moving. So me opening up and expressing myself in a relationship so my significant other can really know me (which would leave me very vulnerable) seemed like it would be a very daunting task (my wife tells me that it took a while for me to really open up to her so she can get to really know me, even after we were married). And then also my trust of people was not very good when I was younger, growing up the way I did, I seemed to be always on guard to protect myself physically, mentally and or emotionally, so opening myself up to people was very hard, and I seldom did.

So yeah, I really didn't think I had the patience and or the time to be in a serious relationship, I just didn't think I could do it. I mean it's like, I remember when we were teenagers my brother had a girlfriend, and I remember how they seem to be always on the phone talking about absolutely nothing, just wasting time on the phone. I thought that was a waste of time. And then, my brother stopped coming to the basketball court with me and our other friend, why, because his girlfriend wanted him to go hang out with her, you know, go to the movies, or the mall, or something like that. I mean, she had him abandon basketball and us for her, I thought that was crazy, and we teased him a lot about it and told him he was whipped. But then a crazy thing happened, our friend got himself a girlfriend that following summer! So there they were, both of them got girlfriends and therefore they both stopped going to the basketball court with me, smh, they straight abandoned me. But I told myself I'm not going to allow myself to fall into their situation and get a girlfriend who will take me away from basketball, especially since I had NBA hoop dreams.

But then another crazy thing happened that summer. I was sitting outside at the back of our building with one of our friends from the same building and we saw these two girls walking coming towards our building, I recognized one of the girls (we went to elementary school together, and I remember she thought she was the most prettiest girl around, I mean she was cute but definitely not the most prettiest, lol), but my eyes were stuck at her friend. Her friend was very pretty, and I mean very very pretty. So as they got closer to us, walking towards our building about to pass us to go inside, I said "Hey, how you guys doing!?" They didn't respond, acting like they didn't hear me, they just walked right past us and went inside the building. But not long after they went inside they came right back out and started walking past us again to leave. They pretended not to notice us again as they passed right by us, but I once again said "Hey, what's up, how you guys doing!?" But once again they didn't say anything, just ignored us. Then I said "Hey, isn't it kinda rude not to respond to someone saying hi to y'all?" And that's when the very pretty girl I was staring at stopped for a few seconds, turned around and said "We don't talk to strangers". Then she turned back around, her and her friend laughed as they started walking away again. But I replied "That's why I said hi, so I can get to know you, so we won't be strangers anymore!" The pretty girl stopped again, turned around, stared at me up and down (like she was sizing me up), then turned around and her and her friend started laughing and walked away. But then about a few days later, me and my friend were sitting in the lobby of our apartment building just chilling talking to the receptionist when my friend says "Hey, look who is coming our way!?" I turned to look and guess who it was? It was the pretty girl from the other day who dissed me hard. She was by herself and she was coming straight to us. We just stared at her as she got closer and closer to us. I was just staring at her and she was looking at the receptionist and then looking at us, back and forth like that, and then when she got right next to us she set right next to me, stared at me for a few seconds, then looked at my basketball which I was holding (I almost always had my basketball with me back in those days, teenage days), then she took the basketball from me, tossed the ball up and down to herself for a few seconds, then asked me if I play ball. I said yes, then she asked me where, I told her, then she said the next time I go play to let her know, I said okay, then she asked to see my hand, I showed it to her, then she proceeded to write her phone number on my hand (this was in the late nineteen eighties and early 90s, way before cell phones), told me her name, and I told her my name, then she got up and walked away, and me and my friend looked at each other like wow, what just happened! I'm telling you, it was so surreal, it was like a movie scene, it was like it was scripted. I can remember it like it was just yesterday, but this was about 30 years ago, when I was about 15 or 16 years old, and afraid of relationships, lol.

And so the next day I called her and asked her if she wanted to go play basketball, she said yes, then came over to my building and we walked together to the basketball court. The basketball court was at this Junior High School in south west D.C., close to the hood. Now, where me and her lived was middle class, but the hood was just about two blocks away, and hearing gunshots every once in a while was not uncommon. I liked playing at the Junior High because it was safer, but once in a while the neighborhood thugs and drug dealers would come to that court to play and check out the games. On those days the games would get extra rough and you had to be alert in case any fights broke out, you know, that way you can either run or be ready to throw down (fight). So when me and the pretty girl were walking to the court I was praying that the thugs wouldn't be there, because I knew they would get rowdy and try to come on to her (try to holler at her) and or harass her, and I would be left with no choice but to defend her honor (fight). But thank God the thugs weren't there that day and me and the pretty girl got to enjoy some pretty good games with no incidents. Now let me tell you, that girl could actually play, I mean she was a real baller, I was very impressed at how good she really was. And when I say good, I don't mean just good enough for a girl, no, she was good enough to play with the boys, she could contend with the boys, she could dribble real good, shoot real good, and even play good defense (she played for her High School basketball team). I was very impressed with her basketball abilities, and I could feel myself starting to develop some strong feelings for her. I could feel the love thing start to penetrate in my heart, and it was happening very fast.

After that day we ended up being almost inseparable. That whole summer we pretty much spent most of the time together, playing ball, working out (we had a fitness center in my apartment building and she would come over and work out with me) or just chilling and talking about life and such. The girl was real cool, her personality was very enjoyable, she had a very infectious laugh, and she loved to smile, and she would force me to smile even if I didn't feel like it, she had a real positive outlook on life, she believed if you focused and worked hard you can achieve anything you want in this world. She was an optimist, and so was I. She had huge dreams and aspirations, and so did I. I couldn't believe that I had met a girl that not only was very pretty, and very smart, but she also loved basketball as much as I did. That was awesome, because back in those days, basketball was my life.

So there I was, enjoying a wonderful summer hanging out with a beautiful girl who loved to play basketball, I was overjoyed. But then summer was coming to an end and she told me that she will have to leave soon to go back home to her mom and get ready to go back to school. You see, she was only there for the summer. I couldn't believe it, I couldn't believe that I actually met a girl that I wouldn't have minded trying the boyfriend girlfriend thing, but she was about to be gone in about a week. I remember I started panicking and sadness started creeping inside of me. But then she told me that her and her mom didn't live that far away (they lived about an hour or so away), which was a relief, because it meant she was still close enough for me to go see her if I wanted to. But I was still feeling kinda sad that I won't be able to see her everyday like I had been able to that whole summer. I'm telling you, that whole final week before she had to leave I was walking around with a heavy heart, missing her already. That's when I knew that I had really fallen for her, and that's when I decided maybe I should go ahead and tell her how much I really like her and maybe we should be boyfriend and girlfriend. So that final week I spent most of the time when I was with her trying to talk myself into revealing to her how much I really liked her. And let me tell you, I was so scared, I mean I was straight out terrified! And the reason why I was so scared is because I wasn't totally sure how she actually really felt about me, you know, like, did she really really like me or did she just like me as a friend. And the other reason why I was so scared is because I just wasn't good at expressing emotions, you know, especially when it came to that love stuff, you know what I mean?

I mean it was crazy, I just couldn't get myself to start the "I like you a lot" conversation. I just couldn't figure out how to do it. But then the weekend when she had to leave had arrived. I think she had to leave on a Saturday or Sunday, but I remember the day before she had to leave we were sitting outside my building, I was dribbling the basketball between my legs back and forth, we weren't really talking much, but I remember she kept asking me if I was okay, I think she sensed my nervousness. But I had told myself, I have to do it, one way or another, I have to find the courage to let her know how I really felt about her, because if I didn't, I may lose the chance of having a girlfriend who seems to be perfect for me. So there we were, sitting very close to each other, not saying much at all, then I decided this is it, it's time to do it, it's time to reveal to her how much I really liked her. So, nervous as heck, with my heart beating real fast and hard, feeling like it's about to burst out of my chest, I finally found the courage to tell her that I really really liked her and that I think we should be boyfriend and girlfriend. I don't really remember what were the exact words that I said, but it was to that effect. But I do remember how she turned and looked at me for a few seconds (without saying anything), then she looked away and looked down (like she was thinking), then she lifted up her head and turned and looked at me and slowly she said "I'm sorry, I don't think that would be a good idea". I could feel panic and devastation overcoming me, as I asked her why. She said she didn't think it would be a good idea because boyfriend and girlfriend relationships tended not to work out and she didn't want to lose me as a friend. She said she really really liked me but she didn't want to chance us not making it as boyfriend and girlfriend thereby we would have to break up and in the process we would lose our friendship.

Wow, what an explanation huh! I was speechless, I didn't know what to say. Because truth be told, most boyfriend and girlfriend relationships usually don't last, and when the couple breaks up, usually their friendship also comes to an end. So there I was, sitting there close next to her, speechless not knowing what to say, trying to digest what she just said. Because on one hand what she said made a lot of sense (I too wouldn't want to lose our friendship), but on the other hand, we would lose the chance to know if we were meant to be together (serious relationship) or not. In my mind I was thinking we should take a chance, but then she asked me if I understood what she said and if her explanation made sense, and I said yes. And so that was it, we would be just friends, which left me with mixed emotions.

The next day I went with her to the bus station (I think it was Greyhound), it was just me and her, and I waited with her till her bus was ready to board. I don't remember what we talked about as we waited, but I remember she gave me the biggest hug ever when time to board came. Then she asked me if I was okay, I said yes, then she said she's gonna call me when she gets home, then she went to board the bus. I stood there watching her get on the bus thinking to myself, "wow, what a great girl, maybe I may still have a chance to be her boyfriend one of these days". As the bus started to drive off she waved bye to me from her seat and I waved back. I stood there for a few extra minutes watching the bus drive away, then I left the station and went home. She called me that evening when she got home. I don't remember what we talked about, but after that we would talk on the phone every once in a while. I remember I spent that whole fall and then spring of the following year waiting for summer to come around so we could hang and see each other everyday again.

I don't really remember what happened that following summer, all I remember is me and her sitting next to each other on the sideline at the basketball court at the junior high that we liked to play at, and as we watched other people play, I remember me telling her that I had to leave the U.S. and go back home to Africa (I was born in Africa, came to the U.S. when I was 11 years old, and I grew up in D.C.). She asked me for how long, I told her I'm not sure (I had a personal issue that required me to have to leave the U.S. and I wasn't sure if I was going to return). I remember she was looking kinda sad and said "don't tell me you are leaving me". I told her sorry there's nothing I can really do, I have to leave. I don't really remember what happened after that, but about a month later I was back home in Africa.

I remember sitting there at my aunt's house in Dar es salam, Tanzania thinking "okay, it's time to learn how to live an African life again", lol. And what I mean by this is that, I had pretty much had become Americanized by then, you know, culturally, economically and such, you know, lifestyle differences. But then about two week later one of my cousins took me to a gymnasium where they were playing basketball and I was impressed. You see, basketball was not really a thing when I was younger growing up in Africa, no, it was only played in prestigious areas of the country and or colleges that were sponsored by foreigners (white foreigners). When I was growing up soccer was the most popular sport in Africa (it still is), but nowadays basketball is becoming big, it's really growing. But so anyway, there I was, at this nice size gymnasium, filled with high school and college age Africans playing basketball, and I thought to myself "okay, alright, maybe my transition to living life in Africa again won't be too bad " lol.

So as I stood there watching them play basketball, I asked my cousin if I could play there, and he said yes, I just need to get a gym membership. And I said okay, and we planned on coming back the next day to pay for the membership. But, as we were walking back home, we saw some guys playing basketball at a small playground. I asked my cousin if we could stop by and check them out and he said sure. So we walked closer to the court and stood there watching. Then some of them asked us if we wanted to play, my cousin said he doesn't play, then he looked at me and said "you can go and play", so I did. I had fun playing with my African brothers and they were kinda good. I think we were playing 21 or 15 (you know, every man for himself, where you try to get the rebound and score). And I think I won, because I kinda remember when we got home my cousin told my aunt (his mom) that I played basketball and I won. But so anyway, after we were done playing and as we were about to leave, some of the players asked me if I would like to join their basketball team (apparently some of them played for a semi-pro basketball team that practiced at that same court that we played on), and I said sure, that would be great. Then they told me when their next practice would be and said I should come and they would introduce me to their coach. I was so excited, I couldn't wait to come back and see about joining their team. But then my cousin said he knows another team that he thought I would like more, and he knew a girl that played for the ladies team in the same organization that could introduce me to the men's team coach. I was like okay, I would love to check them out. So the next day he took me to this basketball court that was about 5 or 10 minutes from the beach (I kid you not), it was nice, and you could feel the ocean breeze and you could hear the ocean waves from the court, it was fantastic.

So there we were (me and my cousin) standing near the basketball court with hundreds of other people watching a basketball game going on. The place was electric, with people really into the game, screaming, shouting, yelling, clapping and such, it was amazing. I remember standing there thinking "yes, yes, yes, I hope I get to play here". After the game my cousin introduced me to the girl that played for the ladies team and told her that I play basketball and asked her if she could introduce me to the men's team coach. She said sure and walked us to where the men's coach was and introduced me and told the coach that I play basketball and that I'm interested in joining the team. The coach asked me a few questions and then invited me to come join them in their next practice and he'll let me know if he thought I was good enough to be part of the team. So at their next practice I showed up and proceeded to practice with them. I had a lot of fun practicing with them, especially with having the beach so close by that I could literally feel the ocean breeze as we practiced, that was amazing. After practice the coach took me to see the general manager, they talked for a few minutes, then the general manager asked me a few questions, then he asked me my jersey size, then added my name to the roster and welcomed me to the team. I was so excited, I was elated!

I had joined the team towards the end of their season, because before I knew it, it was playoff time. I did not get a lot of playing time, I'm guessing because I was new to the team and at 16 years old I was pretty much the youngest player on the team, going against other players in their 20s and 30s. But I did get enough playing time to have fun and enjoy myself on the court. It was amazing, especially when the ladies team would be watching and would start cheering for me almost every time I got in the games. I kid you not, I would hear them on the sideline spelling out my name in a cheer and calling out my name. That was amazing, I had a lot of fun. But the season came to an end too quickly, because before I knew it we were in the championship game. I did not get a lot of playing time in the championship game and I was kinda mad, because the point guard from the other team was killing us with layups and I believed I could have done a better job guarding him. But it is what it is and we ended up losing the game. And you won't believe who beat us, it was the team that had invited me to come join them that time when I went to the gymnasium and then saw them playing at a little playground court. I remember thinking to myself after we lost the championship game and they were handing out the trophies, I was thinking "man, I should have joined that team, I would have been a champion". But, I probably would not have had as much fun as I did being with the team that I was with, especially with our home court being next to the beach, and even more especially with all that attention I was getting from the ladies team, lol. Anyway, the season came to an end and I couldn't wait till the next season started. I was so looking forward to the next season.

A week or so after the basketball season ended I traveled to the village to see my mom, I hadn't seen her in about 5 years. And the funny thing is, nobody really knew exactly where she lived, they only knew the town and the hospital that she worked at. So what happened was, they bought me a bus ticket that headed to one town and then they told me when I got there to ask for the bus that went to the town where the hospital was, and then when I get to that town to ask for the hospital and how I could get there. That was some fun adventure for my 16 year old self who had just come back to Africa from America not that long ago, lol. I felt like I was a tourist on a lone exploration of Africa and trying not to get lost (this was way before Google and cell phones were a thing). But I was up to the task (I like adventures), I was able to navigate to the town where the hospital where my mom worked was at. When I got out of the bus, I walked to this small store and started asking how I can get to the hospital (this was way before uber, lol). One guy that was there asked me why I needed to go to the hospital and I told him that my mom worked there and I had come to visit her. He asked me who my mom was, I told him her name and he stared at me for a long few seconds. To my surprise and luck, not only did he know my mom but he also knew where she lived. So he offered to give me a ride, which I gladly accepted. Before he drove me to my mom's place he invited me for some food at his place. He had a nice house, I remember sitting at the dining room table looking around in amazement and wondering what he did for a living (I didn't ask). The food was delicious, and then his wife brought out some pineapples for dessert, and let me tell you, those pineapples were so sweet I can still taste them right now about 30 years later, lol. After we ate he drove me to my mom's place. My mom was still at work, so he introduced me to her neighbor and the neighbor said my sister (younger sister) had gone to the market and she should be back soon. So I chilled with the neighbor for a little bit till my sister got home. When she got home the neighbor told my sister that I'm her brother. My sister stared at me real good, trying to recognize me from the pictures of me she had seen. Then my sister let me in the house and showed me where I could lay down (because I was exhausted), and I quickly passed out asleep.

A few hours later while still kinda asleep I had a feeling like someone was staring at me. So I slowly opened my eyes and looked up, and yes, someone was staring at me, and it was my mom. She looked shocked, she hadn't seen me in about 5 years and apparently she didn't know that I was coming. The neighbors told me that she almost passed out when she first saw me there asleep. She couldn't stop staring at me, she couldn't believe how big I had gotten from the last time she had seen me when I was 11 years old (I was 16 when she saw me again). I enjoyed living in the village with my mom and little sister, there wasn't much to do but I enjoyed the peacefulness and easy going style of life. The people were really nice, and my mom enjoyed showing me off to the neighbors, who had a hard time believing that I was really her son (my mom has always looked pretty young), they kept insisting that I was her brother and that me and my mom were playing tricks on them.

I was really starting to get used to village life, I was liking the whole lifestyle of farming and raising chickens. So much so that I was actually starting to plan how I would go about starting the farming thing. And I was planning that I would live in the city during basketball season and play basketball and then after the season is over I would live in the village and do the farming thing. I mean, I'm telling you, I was really starting to plan out my African life, the village farming lifestyle had really intrigued me and I was looking forward to it. But a few weeks later (I had been at the village for about a month at this point) my mom came back from work with a letter in her hand that said I had to leave and go back to the city asap because there was a plane ticket waiting for me to go back to America. I couldn't believe it, I was in shock, I didn't know what to think, and I had a lot of mixed emotions about having to leave my mom and little sister and to leave the village. I mean, I was in the midst of planning out my African life, you know, my dream of playing basketball and living in the village as a farmer. Then my mom said there's a bus that leaves for the city in 2 days, and I was not excited about it at all. I mean, I am telling you, I was very distraught about it. I remember thinking maybe I should just turn down the opportunity to return to America. But then I started thinking about the chance to see the girl that I was in love with that I had left in America and the decision to turn down the opportunity became extra hard. Because I mean, even though leaving my mom and sister would be hard, and even though giving up playing semi pro basketball would be hard, I couldn't imagine giving up the chance to see the girl that I was in love with again. I mean, thinking about seeing her again pretty much made my decision to go ahead and come back to America, because otherwise I really didn't have a lot of other motivations to come back to America, especially since I could still chase my basketball dreams from Africa. So yes, I came back to America because of a girl, because of love, lol.

And so anyway, two days later I had to say bye to my mom and sister and some neighbors and got on the bus heading back to the city (Dar es salaam).   I remember sitting on the bus teary eyed thinking maybe I should just get off the bus and forget about America.   But every time I thought about seeing the girl again I got excited, because I kept thinking to myself "what if", what if she feels the same about me as I feel about her and we end up together, how great would that be.   So my decision to go back to America was so I can see about the "what if", you know, so I wouldn't have any regrets of not knowing if me and her were meant to be together or not, I don't like leaving "what ifs" hanging, you know what I mean?

I got to the city the same day at night time, then a few days later my cousin took me to the airport to board my flight back to America. I remember on our way to the airport we drove by the basketball court where I played basketball with the team by the beach, and I remember feeling kinda sad that I was gonna miss the next season that I was looking forward to playing in.

I remember my cousin asking me if I was excited about going back to America, I don't remember what I told him but I remember that I had a lot of mixed emotions about leaving Africa, it was extremely hard to do.

When I got back to America I quickly started searching for the girl's number, but I couldn't find it, but I did find her grandma's number and I called it.   Her grandma remembered me and gave me the girl's number.   I right away called her and I was so happy to hear her voice.   She seemed happy to know that I was back, and I believe she said not to leave her again (if my memory serves me correctly, which it usually does, lol).   We would talk on the phone on and off, I don't really remember what we really talked about but I quickly found out that she had a boyfriend.   I was a little disappointed that she had a boyfriend but I couldn't be too mad about it because for one, we were just friends when I left for Africa (I was gone for about 8 months, and   I wasn't sure if I was coming back), and for two, I'm the one who left instead of staying and fight for her love, you know, work to convince her that she should take a chance and give me a chance to be her boyfriend.   So I wasn't too mad when I found out she had a boyfriend (she's the one who told me) and I wasn't too surprised, because she is a very pretty girl, there's no way she didn't have a lot of boys wanting to be with her.

And so I wasn't too surprised that she had a boyfriend. I was disappointed, but I wasn't mad about it.   We did talk on the phone from time to time, I don't remember what we really talked about, but

I do remember her complaining about her boyfriend and I do remember me telling her that she needs to dump him because he didn't deserve her. I don't remember anything else between me and her in those High School days (we lived in different towns), all I remember is after High School she went to play basketball at a college somewhere and I went to the military. You see, after I came back to America from Africa I decided to switch from basketball to playing football, and the reason for it is because my second growth spurt never came and I never got anywhere close to six feet tall (that was my basketball height aim, which I figured would have made my NBA dreams potential more realistic, I try to be realistic sometimes, lol). So I switched to football, which I really enjoyed and I showed great potential in it. But, the injury thing got me, yeah, I got hurt in my first year of playing football and I never recovered. I mean, I'm telling you, I couldn't believe it. I mean there I was, my first year of actual organized football (I always wanted to play football, and people used to tell me I should try playing football, because I was kinda stocky, you know, muscular) and I was attending a High School that was known as a football school in D.C. And I had purposely chosen to go to that school so I could be in a good football program where college scouts tended to come to check out the players (I'm always masterminding, lol). But it was not to be, I got hurt a few games into the season and I spent the rest of that year on the sidelines trying to recover. That following summer I had surgery, the doctor said I should recover in about 3 weeks or so and I should be able to get back to football. But it was not my luck, because I ended up getting an infection after the surgery and 3 weeks turned into a whole summer of me sitting on the couch watching tv barely able to walk trying not to get too depressed realizing that my football dreams may have just come to an end before I even really had a good chance of pursuing it.

So that following school year I decided to transfer to my neighborhood school so that way I can at least be at a school where my friends where (because I did not know any of the kids at the football school, it was not my neighborhood school, I really just went there so I could play football at a school that was known to be a football school) you know, so I could at least have a little fun hanging out with my friends at school since I was still not physically healthy enough to play any sports. I was in the 11th grade at this time, and not playing any sports for the first time since I can remember was very weird and I was kinda lost and kinda depressed. But, I did start socializing with girls more, you know, and I started to think maybe I should get a girlfriend, you know, since I had all this extra free time. But my macking game wasn't really that good and I was kinda picky at the same time, you know, I didn't want to just hook up or get with any girl, no, I wanted someone special, someone like the girl that I came back to America for. But that was hard to find, or maybe I just didn't give them a chance. Because there were a few girls that kinda liked me but I didn't reciprocate. I don't know what it was, but it seemed like the girls that I kinda liked didn't seem to be into me and the ones I wasn't into seemed to be into me. It was kinda weird, and since my macking and confidence levels were not that up yet, I did not know how to navigate through all that High School flirting stuff. But there was this one girl that I had a real crush on, she played softball and volleyball, and she was real smart (my type) and very pretty (my type again, lol). I remember I used to flirt with her a little bit, but I was so scared to ask her out and or tell her that I really like her. But one day I decided to let her know that I really like her by writing her a note and putting it on her locker. I don't really remember what I wrote, but this was way before cell phones, and writing love notes was kinda a thing at that time, lol.

So the next day I saw her by her locker and walked up to her and asked her if she got my note. She said yes, then said she liked it but her dad does not allow her to have a boyfriend. So that was that, I don't really remember the rest of my High School years. Oh wait, actually I do remember asking her if she would go to the prom with me in our senior year, but I had waited till there was only two weeks left before prom to ask her, and by then someone else had already asked her and she told me she had already said yes to the other person, and I was devastated. I couldn't believe I had missed the chance of going to the prom with her because I had waited too long to ask her. And the reason why I took so long to ask her was because I was so scared, and so I procrastinated almost a whole month before I mustered enough courage two weeks before prom, which turned out to be too late. I remember being so mad with myself that I didn't even go to the prom. And I remember telling myself that next time I find myself so into a girl I won't procrastinate too long in telling her how I feel about her, you know, so I won't miss out on a chance to be with someone special, so I won't miss out on potential love.

And so anyway, after High School I went to the military (Army). There's three reasons why I really went to the military, one is because when I was younger I thought being a soldier was really cool, so it was kinda a dream of mine that I wanted to experience. And two: to get some of that GI Bill (money for college). And three: which is the bigger reason, I wanted to see if I could rehab my injury and be healthy and fit enough again to get back to playing football. I had figured that four years of military physical training might give my injury more time to heal while getting me fit. But it wasn't to be, I just couldn't get my injury to heal all the way. I mean, there's always been some discomfort that doesn't seem to ever go away. I thought maybe I should try getting back to basketball, but it had been almost 3 years since I had played any real organized basketball. So slowly I started to realize that my dreams of chasing an athletic career were pretty much over and I had to think of what other dreams and or goals in life I may want to pursue. While I was trying to think and plan my future after the military (I knew I wasn't going to make the military my career), I found myself socializing more and more with the ladies of that wonderful military town and city that was close to the base (I was stationed in Fort Hood, Texas), nothing serious, just doing my little single life dating thing and running away from any situation that seemed to look like it may be getting serious, you know what I mean, lol.

And so time went by, and before I knew it I had only one more year left in my military tour before I could get out and be back in the civilian world again. And in the beginning of my last year I had one week of vacation time that I could use before I got out of the military, so I decided to go to D.C. for the week. And when I got there I decided to see if I could get in touch with the girl that I had been in love with all these years, but we were just friends. I did not have her number, so I called her grandma again, and her grandma gave me her number and I quickly called her. To my surprise she was actually living in D.C., she was attending college at one of the universities in D.C. I was so excited, I couldn't believe she was actually in D.C., I thought to myself that this must be fate, and I couldn't wait to go see her. So she gave me her address and the next day or so I went to see her. And as soon as I saw her all those feelings that I had for her came running right back into my heart, and I knew that I was still in love with her. I don't really remember much of what we talked about that day, but I do remember that we went down to Georgetown (D.C.) by the water and got some ice cream and sat down and talked for a good while.

I remember just looking at her the whole time and thinking to myself, wow, what a great lady she is, not only beautiful and smart but also very pleasant to be around. I remember thinking how wonderful it would be if I actually ended up being with her, how lucky a man I would be. Then I decided, you know what, I need to go ahead and shoot my shot again and let her know that I still have strong feelings for her and that I think we belong together. So I decided before that day was over I'm gonna ask her to take a chance on us and see if we could have something special being together in a serious relationship. So that evening we went back to her dorm room and we did some more talking. All the while I was just looking for an opportune time to shoot my shot and reveal that I still have strong feelings for her. But then she started to ask me about my plans after I get out of the military and I told her that I was seriously thinking about getting into the music business. You see, I always loved music, and I used to write little poetry here and there from when I was younger, and I always thought about writing songs, but it wasn't until I was in the military and realizing that my sports dreams were pretty much over that I started seriously thinking about chasing a music career. So when she asked me my plans after the military I already knew that chasing a music career would be it. Then she asked me what kind of music I wanted to make, and I told her hip-hop and r&b. And then she asked me why I don't make gospel music. I paused for a few seconds, and I told her that truthfully I really didn't know much about gospel music or the gospel industry, plus I really love hip-hop. Then she told me I could do gospel hip-hop and that it was really coming up (Kirk Franklin was really starting to blow up around this time). I remember sitting there in her dorm room thinking to myself why she is strongly trying to push me into gospel music instead of hip-hop and r&b. But then she revealed to me that she had recently gotten Saved, meaning she had recently gotten baptized and accepted Jesus Christ as her Lord and Savior and that she was now more of a church girl and was more into gospel music instead of circular music. I mean wow, she really caught me off guard with that revelation, I didn't know what to think. And I mean I'm a Christian myself, and I used to go to church more often than not, but I guess I wouldn't be considered a church boy, especially since I was so circular.

And so there I was, in her dorm room, waiting for a chance to shoot my shot again and tell her that I think we should be together, but before I could, she reveals to me that she's a church girl now, letting me know that she's not into all that circular music stuff anymore, which would mean for me to actually have a shot of being with her I probably would have to become a church boy. I remember sitting there in her dorm room kinda speechless, not sure what to do or say, just thinking to myself "oh no, I don't think shooting my shot at this point would be a good idea, I'll just have to wait and see if the universe will give me another chance to shoot my shot with her down the road, and or maybe I will learn how to become a church boy down the road and increase my chance of being with her". But then she revealed to me that there's a young man at her church who seemed to really like her, but she wasn't sure if she should give him a chance or not. So I asked her why she was not sure, and she said because he was a little bit younger than her. So I asked her how much younger, and she said about two years younger. Then I asked her if she really liked him, and she said yes she thinks she does. Then I asked her if he seemed to be a very mature person, and she said yes. Then I paused for a few seconds thinking to myself, if I tell her to give him a chance that would probably be the end of me having any chance to be with her. But then I thought, since the guy is a church boy, he may be more evenly yoked (match better) with her than me and her, since I wasn't a church boy and the chances of me becoming a church boy any time soon would be hard to imagine, with me being so circular at the time. And so I went ahead and told her that she should give the guy a chance, two years is not that much of an age gap, especially if the guy seems to be very mature. And then she looked at me and gave me a big hug, and I knew at that moment that my journey to love would have to continue elsewhere, as she would no longer be available for me to think that I still had a chance to be with her, as I had a feeling that if the guy turned out to be a nice guy, they would most likely end up marrying each other sooner than later. I really felt it, I just had a feeling that she was about to be off the market, you know, no longer available to be pursued. But I was ok with it, because if the guy turned out to be the one for her and made her happy, then I would be very happy for her, because she is a wonderful person, and she deserved to find love and happiness, even if it wasn't with me.

So at the end of the night when it was time for me to leave, we hugged and she gave me this very nice teddy bear, which I took back to the military with me and placed it on my bed. It stayed on my bed for a long while, until one day I had to take it off my bed and place it in my closet because I had a lovely Texas young lady coming to visit me and I didn't want to have to explain why there's a teddy bear in my bed, lol.

And so anyway, I did my best to try not to get in trouble with the ladies in that lovely Texas military town, especially since I only had one more year before I was done with the military. And what I mean by trouble is, not getting caught up and or breaking hearts. But those Texas ladies just wouldn't leave me alone, lol. And one of them almost ended up turning me into a step daddy, smh. See what had happened was, we were supposed to be just chilling (just dating, nothing serious), then next thing I know I started getting used to being around her and her kids. She had two young children, a son who was about 8 and a daughter who was about 6 years old. I remember her daughter was starting to get really attached to me, so much so that every time I would come around to their place, as soon as she would see me she would call out my name and she would run to me and jump into my arms and proceed to give me the biggest hug in the world. And then she would sit next to me and start asking me a million questions. She was a sweet and cute little girl. And I remember thinking to myself, where is her father? It was obvious to me that she needed and or wanted a father figure in her life, but I knew I was not anywhere close to being ready to not only be a father (have children), but definitely not ready to be a step-dad. So I knew I would have to end things with her mom sooner than later, because the more I stayed with her mom the more the little girl would get used to me, and when me and her mom would finally end things, I knew the little girl's heart would be broken as well, because she was starting to get really used to seeing me on the weekends. And actually I too was starting to get used to seeing the little girl on the weekends, because she was so happy to see me and seeing her happy brought joy into my heart. And her mom was real cool, just so real, what you see is what you get kinda person, she didn't mince words, you didn't have to guess what kind of mood she was in or what she was thinking because she just told it like it is, whether you liked it or not, she didn't play around, she was kinda hood and classy at the same time. I remember her telling me that she used to be in a gang when she was younger, then she realized she had to straighten her life out (so she can better care for her children) and went back to school and became a nurse. She was really cool, and I kinda started falling for her, but I knew I was nowhere ready to be a step-dad and so I decided I needed to find a way to end it sooner than later.

So one day I called her and told her that I was planning to go back to D.C. when I get out of the military (which was less than a year away). I remember her asking me if I was planning on leaving her, and I remember saying no, and I remember telling her that she is welcome to move to D.C. if she wants to. But she said no, she doesn't want to leave Texas. I don't really remember what happened after our that conversation, but I remember we started not calling each other much and then one day she called me and said that one of her baby daddies is coming back to Texas from Korea in a few weeks (he was a soldier) and wanted to get back with her when he got back (I guess they had kinda broken up). I remember her telling me that she wasn't sure if she wants to get back with him, and I remember telling her that since he's the father of one of her children (not sure if he was the father of the son or daughter, she told me which but I can't remember) I don't think it would be such a bad idea to give him another chance, because if it works out that would be good for the kids, as they would have a father figure in their lives. After that conversation our association kinda naturally ended, I think we just stopped calling each other, it was weird, we just stopped calling each other.

I decided after that association ended that I was done dating until I got out of the military and was back in D.C., because I just didn't want any more troubles with the ladies. But, one weekend as I was just chilling in my room watching sports, a military buddy of mine called and said he was doing a little grilling at his house and I should come over and eat and chill. So I said okay cool and I drove over to his place. When I got there he said let's go to Blockbuster and get some movies (this was way before Netflix, and Blockbuster was the best video store to rent movies from). I said okay cool, and we went. As soon as we went inside he tapped me on the shoulder and said turn to your right and look. So I turned to my right and looked. And then I turned back to him and we both said "wow". And why did we say "wow"? It's because there was a very sexy lady standing to our right who was very blessed, you know, very blessed with what her mama gave her, and this was way before butt implants had become popular, lol. There she was, standing facing away from us, then walking back and forth checking out the movies to see what she wants to rent. We stood there for a few more seconds appreciating her sexiness and then I started walking away. But before I walked any farther my friend grabbed me by my shoulder and said "don't tell me you are not gonna try to get her number". I said nah, I'm good. Then he said "what, don't tell me you're gonna let all that sexiness pass you by". I said, I'm good, I'm not trying to mess with any ladies at the moment. He then looked at me and said, "don't tell me you're scared, because if I wasn't married I would be all over that". I remember just looking at him and laughing. He was a wild and cool white boy, who loved him some black ladies. But his wife was white, but he had some wandering eyes for black ladies. Matter fact I remember him telling me that he was having some extra curricular activities with this black female sergeant that was in a different unit than us. I remember every time the female sergeant would walk by and we would see her he would go and say something to her and I would look at their interaction and they seemed very friendly with each other. And I remember thinking to myself that "this dude is wild, he out here messing around when he got a beautiful wife at home (his wife looked like a supermodel, I kid you not, and she was real nice, every time I went to their place she was very friendly and asked me how I was doing and all that) with two young children. I remember telling him on more than one occasion that if he's not careful he's gonna end up messing things up with his wife, but he was one of those kinds of people you just couldn't tell them anything, you know, they do what they want.

But anyway, there we were at Blockbuster Video and he started to challenge me to go talk to the sexy lady if I wasn't scared. Then he bet me ten dollars that I won't go talk to her. So me being a sucker for a challenge I said okay get your ten dollars ready, and I walked to go talk with the sexy lady. When I got close to her I said "Hi, how you doing?" She turned around slowly and looked at me and said "fine". I don't remember the rest of the conversation but she ended up writing her number on a piece of paper and giving it to me. I said bye and walked towards where my friend was standing and showed him the number. He couldn't believe that not only I went to talk to her but that she actually gave me her number. I couldn't believe she actually gave me her number either. We both agreed that she probably gave me a fake number so I could stop talking to her, you know, so I can stop bothering her, lol. So he paid me my ten dollars that we betted and we got us a movie and we headed back to his place to eat and chill.

The next day I was just chilling in my room and I started thinking maybe I should call the number that the sexy lady at Blockbuster gave me and see if it was real or not. So I went ahead and dialed the number on my phone and low behold, she actually gave me her real number. I panicked for a few seconds when she answered, while thinking to myself, what am I doing, I'm not supposed to be doing any dating at the moment. But her voice on the phone was sounding too sexy and remembering how sexy her body was kept me talking to her on the phone for a long while, and by the end of the conversation she invited me to her place for that following weekend. So when the weekend came I drove to her place and she opened the door and let me in. She led me to the living room and asked me if I wanted something to drink, I think I got a beer. I was never much of a drinker but I used to drink a beer or two for socializing, but after the military I actually stopped drinking any alcohol up to now (over twenty years later). And so, after she gave me a beer she said she was about to finish cooking and asked me what I wanted to watch on TV, and I told her the sports channel would be good. So she put on the TV for me and she would go back and forth between the kitchen and the living room making small conversations while cooking. Then a few minutes later I heard a kid crying in a room, it was her 7 year old son. I remember sitting there thinking, I can't believe I'm about to be dating another woman with kids. She went ahead and tended to her son and introduced me to her son and then took her son to his grandma's house, next door over. She lived in those attached one level houses, where her mom and dad lived in the house to the right and she lived in the middle house and her brothers lived in the house to the left. And so, after she took her son to grandma, she set the table for two and we ate and then chilled by the TV and did some small talk. Then when it got real late she told me I could sleepover if I wanted to, and of course I wanted to. I don't remember how much sleep I got that night but I remember waking up to the smell of breakfast being prepared. I remember thinking, this is cool, I never had a date that cooked me dinner and breakfast, I was appreciating her very much. I remember I ended up staying the whole weekend, and when it was time for me to leave Sunday night I couldn't wait till the following weekend so we could do the whole thing over again.

And when the next weekend came, I went over to her place and we did the whole thing all over again. This time she cooked steak, man I was feeling special. Then I started going over to her place even on the weekdays. Then next thing I know, I had ended up going to her place everyday for a whole month straight, sleeping there and everything. I remember one day my military roommate said to me "hey, do you realize you haven't slept in your bed for a whole month". I couldn't believe it, I looked at my barracks' bed and realized I hadn't slept in it in a long time. Then I started panicking and thought to myself, oh no, what am I doing? I'm not supposed to be hooking up with any ladies at the moment, but here I am playing house with a lady that I know I have no long term interest in. I mean, even though the lady was sexy and treated me good, I knew there was no chance for a long term relationship between me and her, because not only I was not ready to be a step-dad (she had a kid), and not only was I about to get out the military in about 5 months, I had realized that besides the physical thing, we didn't really have much more in common. So I decided it's better I break it off now then play house some more and have her thinking there's a chance for a long term relationship between me and her, because we were actually just supposed to be chilling, you know, nothing serious. But, unbeknownst to me, she had actually started catching real feelings for me and she had started getting really used to me going over to her place and being around her and her people. Her mom actually really liked me, and her brothers were cool with me, but her dad I wasn't sure about, he actually made me kinda nervous every time I saw him, because he hardly said much to me when I tried to say hi to him. Her dad was a military soldier as well, more higher ranking than me, and he hardly spoke to me. I'm guessing he knew that I wasn't up to no good with his daughter, you know, he knew I wasn't serious, or maybe he was waiting to see if I was serious or not before he became cordial with me.

But so anyway, I decided to start pulling back and not go over her place too much, so that way things can start slowing down between me and her, and hopefully things can end kinda smoothly when she realizes my interest in our thing is no longer there. But, things didn't end so well, because once she realized I was trying to end it she got kinda angry and started accusing me of leading her on and stuff like that. I didn't realize that she was actually starting to think there may be potential for a long term relationship between us. I didn't think that she actually liked me a lot. I remember feeling so bad about having to break up with her, and I remember I kept apologizing and telling her that I don't think a long term thing would work between us, especially since I would be going back to D.C. after my military time was done in about 5 months. But she did not take it so well and I felt really bad about it. After we had a big conversation, in which she kept calling me an ass-whole, we didn't speak again for about two weeks, and I was thinking, okay, I guess we are finally done. But then she called me a week after that and said that she is pregnant and I can ask her mother if I don't believe her, because her mother was there when she took the pregnancy test. I don't really remember much after she told me she was pregnant because I started feeling kinda dizzy and I had a big migraine coming on. I remember her asking me if I wanted to speak to her mother to confirm that she was pregnant and I said no. Then she started asking me if I was okay because I didn't sound so good, I could barely speak, my voice was fading. I told her I'm fine, I just need to lay down for a few minutes. Then she started laughing and said she would call me the next day to check on me, and I said okay thank you. I then hung up the phone, got on my bed, laid down, and with my eyes wide open I stared up at the ceiling half dazed thinking to myself, what the heck did I just do. I was laying there in bed with an extremely intense headache and in disbelief that I was so careless and actually ended up impregnating her.

The next day I remember sitting on a couch in my room trying to watch a football game (it was the playoffs) but I had a hard time concentrating, because all I kept thinking was, oh man, I can't believe I'm about to become a baby daddy. Later that evening she called me and asked me if I was ok, I said yes I'm fine. Then she asked me a question that I didn't even anticipate, she asked me if I wanted her to have an abortion or keep the pregnancy. She had caught me off guard with that question, because I hadn't thought of abortion as an option. So I told her it was up to her, whatever she decides I will support her. So of course she decided she was going to keep the pregnancy and I started preparing myself to become the best baby daddy that I could be, lol. But, about two months later she called me in a panic and asked if I could take her to the hospital. So I jumped in my car and quickly drove to her place to pick her up and rush her to the hospital. I then sat at the waiting area in the emergency room while the nurses took her to the back to examine her. Then about an hour or so later she came out looking sad and she told me that she lost the baby, she had a miscarriage. I remember feeling really bad for her, because she seemed to have really wanted the baby. I mean she was even getting me kinda excited about having a kid. We had become friendly after she told me she was pregnant, and we had even started thinking of baby names. But I guess it wasn't meant to be. So I drove her home after the hospital, and we talked a little bit but we didn't have much to say, as I think we both knew that our thing (relationship) had just come to an end. So when we got to her place, she looked at me and said thank you for being there during the pregnancy, then smiled and said "but you are still an ass-whole ". I smiled back and said "sorry it didn't work out". Then she got out of the car and I slowly drove off, and that was the end of that situation.

I remember as I was driving away from her place and back to the military base, all I kept thinking was, oh man, that was close, I almost became a baby daddy. So I said to myself, I have to be more disciplined and not get myself in that kind of situation again, because I never wanted to be one of those guys that had to deal with baby mamas. I always said from when I was younger that, when I'm ready to have kids I want it to be with the woman I marry, you know, my wife, because baby daddy and baby mamas dramas seemed like a lot of work to me, and I never wanted any part of that. But as we all know, it's very easy to become a baby daddy and or a baby mama, so I told myself I have to make sure I'm more disciplined in my dating situations.

And so, after that almost becoming a baby daddy situation had ended, I decided definitely no more dating for me until I get out of the military and I'm back in D.C. I had about three months left before I got out and I used to just chill in my room and watch sports or read a book, and go to the library and read magazines and newspapers on Sunday's (this was way before the internet). But then one Sunday as I was at the library reading the newspaper, in the corner of my eye I saw this lovely young lady walk past me. So I lowered my newspaper a little bit to have a better look at her, and I watched her walk to a copy machine to make some copies. She was gorgeous, and she was wearing daisy dukes (short shorts) and a small top that showed her sexy mid waist, and her legs looked splendid and she walked like a model. I kid you not, I could not stop looking at her. Then my heart did something, it skipped a beat, and then i said to myself, oh no, come on heart, you can't do this to me, I'm not supposed to be dating until i get out the military. Then she moved from the copy machine and walked to an aisle looking for some books. Then my heart skipped a beat again as I watched her walk. Then my heart said "maybe you should go talk to her and see what she's all about". But my brain said "are you crazy, you just came from almost becoming a baby daddy, and you said you are not doing anymore dating till you get out the military, so why are you even entertaining thoughts of talking to her". But my heart said "what if she's the one, what if she turns out to be a very special young lady in your life, wouldn't that be great, are you really gonna let the opportunity to find out pass you by". So I sat there thinking and considering what my heart and my brain were telling me and decided maybe my heart as a stronger point, do I really want to let the chance of finding out if this young lady may be the one or not, especially with how gorgeous she is. Also I was thinking, what are the chances that she would actually give me her phone number. So I decided let me just go and chit chat with her for a few seconds and just at least hear how her voice sounds, you know, see if her voice matched her gorgeousness.

So I got up and walked towards her. She pretended not to notice me until I got real close to her and said "hi, how are you doing". Then without turning to look at me she said "fine". Then I asked her if I could help her find whatever books she was looking for. Then again without turning to look at me she asked me "why, do you know where every book in this library is?" I replied "no, but I wouldn't mind struggling to find whatever books you are looking for". She then kinda smiled, then finally turned to look at me, and then asked me "what is it that you really want from me?" She had caught me off guard with that question, I stood there thinking for a few seconds and then said something like, "whatever you have to offer". Then she said "all I can offer you is friendship". Then I said "that sounds good to me, I'll take it". Then she kinda smiled and looked at me for a few seconds and then turned around and picked up a book from the shelf and just walked away. I didn't know what to do or think, I just stood there watching her as she walked back to the copy machine to make some more copies. Then I decided to just go over and ask her for her phone number and see what would happen. So I went by the copy machine and asked her for her phone number. She turned and looked at me for a few seconds and asked me, "if I give you my number will you stop bothering me?" I said yes, then she wrote a phone number on a piece of paper and gave it to me. I took the piece of paper, said thank you and turned around to walk away. But then I realized I didn't get her name, so I turned back around and asked her name. She told me her name and I told her my name and then I turned around and walked away. I went back to where I was sitting and just watched her as she made copies, and said to myself, I hope she didn't give me a fake number and fake name. Then I watched her walk to the checkout counter, and then I watched her walk out the library. I sat there at the library thinking to myself, oh wow, what a gorgeous young lady, I really hope she didn't give me a fake number. Then that evening when I got back in my room I decided to go ahead and call the number to see if it was real or not. But to my surprise the number was real, I couldn't believe that she had given me her real phone number. I was elated and overjoyed when I heard her voice on the phone. And as we started talking I told her that I was sure she had given me a fake number and asked her why she gave me her real number. She said she actually had intended on giving me a fake number but then just decided to give me her real number, but she wasn't sure why. Then I told her maybe it's fate, you know, fate wouldn't let her give me a fake number. She laughed and said she didn't believe in fate. I don't remember the rest of the conversation from that day but we ended up talking for a while and we actually spoke on the phone almost everyday from that day on. I would call her on the phone everyday in the evening and we would talk for a long time, it reminded me of when my brother had a girlfriend during our teenage years and they would be on the phone for a long time, and I used to wonder how can anyone be on the phone that long, you know, I thought it was a waste of time, how much can two people really have to say to each other, I didn't get it. But, I did get it when I found myself on the phone for hours everyday talking about I don't know what, I can't really remember, but we seemed not to be running out of conversations. It was amazing and I loved how her voice sounded on the phone, especially how she said my name, she had me falling in love with her even before we had gone on any dates yet.

Now, the dating part was kind of a struggle, because she said her mom was kinda strict and had a habit of being all over her dating life, as in being very nosy and asking a million questions whenever she tries to date. So she had decided not to date until she moved out of the house (she lived with just her and her mom). Her mom was in the military and they lived on base. She was a 19 year old college student, and she and her mom didn't seem to be getting along. I think her mom was strict and over protective and she didn't like it. I used to tell her to be patient with her mom because her mom was probably just being over protective because she's a single mother and just trying to do the best parenting job she can. But I was getting kinda frustrated because I really wanted to see her again but she wouldn't let me go see her and or pick her up to go on a date. So one day I asked her why don't she let me come and meet her mom, because moms usually like me. She laughed and said "you haven't met my mom, she doesn't like anybody". Then I asked her why don't she let me come pick her up from school (her college) and drop her home. She liked that idea and said okay, but I couldn't drop her off in front of her house because she didn't want her mom asking her who is that, that dropped you off. But it was a great idea and I actually ended up being able to see her about three times a week (the days she had classes) as I would pick her up after her classes and drive her home.   But that wasn't good enough or adequately satisfying, because the drive from the college to her house was only about 15 minutes (she attended on base college), and she was very strict in having me drive her straight home, no deviating to somewhere else to hang out for a little bit or anything like that.

So one day I told her that I really wanted to take her on a date, and that she might just have to let me meet her mom and see if her mom may take a liking to me, and maybe then we may be able to date without her mom being uneasy about her dating. She said she would think about it, and I said cool. That night we ended up talking very late into the night, and neither one of us seemed to want to hang up the phone. But we eventually were able to hang up the phone and we said goodnight to each other. But then, early that following morning my phone rang and it was her calling me. When I picked up the phone and said hello, she said "hey, my mom just left for work and if you want to come over and give me an early morning visit you can". I couldn't believe my ears, and of course I said yes, that sounds like a good idea. And as soon as I hung up the phone I jumped off my bed, threw some clothes on, splashed some water on my face, grabbed my car key and ran to the car and sped off to her house. I got there in no time, speeding like a mad man (I'm glad there were no cops around, because I was pushing pedal to the metal, lol). When I got to her place I knocked on the door, she opened the door looking very lovely in her nightgown. She then let me in the house and I don't remember us talking much but it was a beautiful morning, lol. But I couldn't stay long because I had to get back to the barracks and to my unit so I can be on time for the daily early morning PT (physical training, running and stuff). I remember rushing out of her place and jumping into my car and speeding back to the barracks. As soon as I got there, I saw that my unit had already gathered and was getting ready to call "attention". I ran like crazy into formation and jumped into my spot just before they called "attention". Then as we were about to start exercising, my roommate asked me where was I, and said that he was worried that I was gonna miss formation and get in trouble. I told him that I had an early morning situation that I had to go see about.   He just looked at me for a few seconds then laughed and said "oh wow, you crazy". I was on cloud nine for the rest of that day, all I kept thinking was "wow, wow wow". I couldn't believe that she had actually invited me over to her place and we actually shared in making the morning beautiful. I was in dreamland that whole day.

Then that evening or the next day she asked me if I was still interested in meeting her mom, and I said yes. So a few days later I went to her place to meet her mom, and I was so nervous. I never really got that nervous about meeting parents of the ladies I dated before, but this time I was extremely nervous, I couldn't believe how nervous I really was. But from how strict she had described her mom was, I'm not surprised at how nervous I was. So when I got to her place, she let me in and showed me a couch to sit on and then called her mom and introduced me to her mom. Her mom actually seemed pretty cool, calm and collected, but there was an air of seriousness about her. Her mom spoke very calmly but assertively, as she asked me some questions about myself and things like that. I don't really remember much of what she asked me, but I do remember her asking me "what is it that you really want from my daughter?" She had caught me off guard with that question, I had no idea what to say. I turned and looked at the other end of the couch at her daughter but her daughter was not trying to make eye contact with me, she just sat there very quietly looking kinda nervous herself, which made me even more nervous. Then I turned to her mom and said something like "I'm not really sure". Then she said "if you are not sure then why are you here". Wow, she had caught me off guard again, I wasn't sure what to say. So I just said that I was trying to get to know her daughter better. Then she asked me "you're not trying to play around with my daughter are you?" I said "no ma'am". I don't really remember what happened after that, but I remember being very uncomfortable the whole time that I was there, and I didn't stay long. I remember driving back to the barracks and to my room not sure if that encounter with her mom went well or not.

I continued talking to the girl on the phone and picking her up from school and driving her home while trying to convince her that she should come hang out with me and go on a date with me. But she was so worried about what her mom would say and things like that. But one day she called me up and asked me if I would like to go on a double date with her and her friend. And of course I said yes. So a few days later I went to pick her up and then we went to pick up her friend and the other guy, and we went to a park that had a lake where some people were fishing and other people were just hanging out. I enjoyed being around her, and I could feel myself starting to fall for her. But she seemed kinda uneasy, like she had a hard time relaxing and enjoying the moment. She seemed kinda tense, and then before you know it she said she had to go home. We didn't stay long at the park at all. So I dropped off her friend and the other guy and drove her home. A few days later I was able to get her to let me go pick her up and come hang out with me at the barracks. She seemed a little bit more relaxed this time, and we chilled in my room for a little bit. But as soon as she seemed to be getting more comfortable she decided it was time for her to go home. I remember thinking why does she seem to be having a hard time relaxing, it's almost like she would catch herself getting comfortable and would kinda panic and make herself uncomfortable and say she had to go. So I drove her back home and on my way back to the barracks I thought to myself that this is gonna be a very hard challenge to get her to relax and enjoy the moments with me.

Another few days later I was able to once again get her to let me pick her up and come hang out with me. I went to pick her up and we drove about 45 minutes to this big park by a waterfront on base that had some boats and amusement park rides. She enjoyed the drive a lot, it was kinda long and it was like driving through the countryside. She seemed a lot more relaxed and really enjoying the drive. I remember she would stick her hand outside the window and do waves and that kind of stuff. I remember just looking at her and thinking to myself, man, I think I'm falling in love with her. So when we got to the place, I parked the car, we got out of the car and started walking down to the amusement park. I remember looking at the place (it was a nice spot for a date) and looking at her and thinking to myself, okay, I think this is going to be a magical date. But, not more than fifteen minutes after we got there she said she had to go home. I remember thinking to myself, what the heck is going on with her, why is it that she always has to leave and go home not long after we get to a place to hang out. I don't remember if I asked her why or if she told me why, all I remember is that I was very disappointed that we didn't get a chance to really hang out, and I had heard that they did fireworks at the place when it got dark, which I was really looking forward to, because it would have set up a real good romantic atmosphere. But, we had to go, so we left.

I don't remember much about the drive back besides me thinking whether or not I was wasting my time chasing her. I remember thinking maybe I should just end it and move on with my life, especially since I only had about two months left before I got out of the military. But I had already fallen for her, something about her just made me want to get to know her even more and even try to be with her seriously. We continued to talk on the phone and I continued picking her up from school. Then one day I asked her again if she would let me pick her up so we could go hang out at the mall and stuff like that. She said okay and I went to pick her up. She looked very lovely that day, she looked like a model, with her model walk. I remember I needed to get an oil change because I had been putting it off, and I asked her if she didn't mind us stopping at the car service place before we went to the mall, and she was fine with it. I remember when we got to the car service place and she got out of the car, the car service people all turned to check her out. And then the guy that was doing my car's oil change told her that she looks so beautiful and she said thank you. Then he turned to me and asked "where did you find her at, because I didn't know there's such beautiful girls in this town". Me and her both laughed. After the oil change we went ahead and drove to the mall. When we got to the mall she seemed nervous about going in. I asked her what's wrong, why she seemed nervous about going in. She said that we might run into people that know her and they may start asking her about me and or may go tell her mom that they saw her at the mall with a guy. I told her she needs to stop worrying too much and try to enjoy the moment. Then we went inside the mall and walked around and did some window shopping. I enjoyed walking around the mall with her and I did end up buying her a dress. I don't remember the rest of that day or the days that followed except for the final week before I was getting out of the military. I don't remember how I told her that I was about to get out of the military, but I do remember inviting her to come visit me in D.C. and see if it's a place she thinks she could move to and live. I remember she was excited about the idea of visiting me in D.C. and checking it out. She had always talked about wanting to leave Texas and go somewhere else, so I figured if she liked the idea of living in D.C. that would pretty much give us the chance to get to know each other even more and see if we can get into a serious relationship and see what that leads to. I was so happy when she accepted my invitation and agreed to come visit me in about two week after I had left. I don't really remember how I said bye to her on my last day in the military, all I remember is after two weeks after I had left she did not come to visit me. I remember calling her multiple times to see what had happened to our plan, but she wouldn't give me clear answers. I remember being so frustrated, because I was so looking forward to her coming to visit me. Then I decided, you know what, I'm gonna go back to Texas to see what's going on with her and or why she's having a change of heart about coming down to D.C. to visit me.

So the following week I booked a round trip ticket and flew back to Texas to go check her out and see why she's having a change of heart. When I landed in Texas one of my military buddies picked me up at the airport and we drove down to his place that was close to the base and I stayed there for the night. The next day my buddy let me use his car to drive to the girl's house to see her. When I got to her place I knocked on the door and she came and opened it. When she saw me she looked very surprised that I had actually come back (I had told her that I was coming, I guess she didn't believe me), as she stood there at the door for a few seconds just staring at me without saying anything. Then she said something like "I can't believe you actually came back". And I said something like "of course I did". Then I asked her if we could go somewhere and talk. But she said she had already made plans to go to the movies with her friend. And I said, "why don't you call her and tell her that I came back and perhaps you guys can reschedule to go to the movies another day, since I have come a long way to see and talk to you". But she said "no, I don't think that is a good idea, I don't want to cancel on her". I remember just standing there outside the door looking at her in disbelief that she wouldn't cancel going to the movies with her friend, after I had traveled such a long way to see her. I started to think to myself, maybe she really doesn't want to mess with me anymore, you know, maybe she doesn't really like me as much as I like her. Because I mean, if she really liked me a lot, she would be pleased that I had traveled a long way to see her and spending time with me would have been a priority over going to the movies with a friend who didn't live that far from her, whom she could see any day after I had left. She really did not give me a warm welcome, I felt she was dissing me. I stood there in disbelief for a few more seconds and decided, okay, she doesn't really want to see me, so let me just get out of here. So I said bye to her and I left. When I got back to my buddies' place he asked me how it went and I told him not good, not good at all. He asked me "So what are you gonna do, are you gonna try to go see her tomorrow or what?" I told him I'm not sure, let me just sleep on it and I'll see how I feel about it tomorrow. The next day I woke up still feeling like she dissed me hard, and I didn't feel like going to see her, so I didn't. I didn't go to see her the following day either, nor the day after that. I ended up not going to see her the whole week that I was there. I just chilled at my buddies' place watching sports all day everyday that whole week, as I was waiting for the day my return flight back to D.C. to arrive. When the day to fly back to D.C. arrived, my buddy drove me to the airport and I boarded the plane and I bid adieu to Texas.

When I got back to D.C. I felt very heart broken, I couldn't believe that she had dissed me like that, I did not see that coming. Then I decided, let me write her a letter and ask her what happened, why did she have a change of heart about coming to visit me in D.C. and why did she diss me like that when I flew back to Texas to see her. To my surprise she actually wrote me back not that long after I had sent her my letter. And she actually wrote me a nice letter saying something like she had panicked when I had flown back to see her and she wasn't sure how to react about it, because she realized that I was serious about her but she wasn't sure if she wanted a serious relationship at the time. She said she had actually followed a guy to his hometown before and the guy treated her badly and she just didn't want to get caught up in that kind of situation again. She said she really liked me but things between us seemed to be moving too fast and she just wasn't ready to be in a serious situation at the moment. Then she said she really doesn't want to fall in love at the moment, nothing personal but falling in love scares her at the moment, and so she would rather not force herself into it, because the negative side of love scares her. She also said she's not sure when she may be ready to take a chance on love again, nothing personal.

I remember reading the letter very slowly, so I could make sure I understood what she was trying to say. And I remember thinking to myself, man, my timing with her was not very good, you know, I came into her life not long enough after she had gone through a bad relationship thing with another guy, so I was paying the price for the other guys' mistreatment of her. And this explains why she never seemed totally relaxed those numerous times I would go pick her up to go hang out with me, it's because she was not really ready to be in a relationship again at that point, and so when she would catch herself starting to feel relaxed and or comfortable with me she would get kinda scared, because she didn't want to catch feelings for me and end up falling in love with me, she was protecting herself emotionally, she just wasn't ready for love at that moment, so it was bad timing on my part. So after the letter I decided to accept my loss of a chance to be with her and just move on with my broken heart. Truth be told, it wasn't easy to move on with my broken heart, I used to miss her tremendously. I used to miss hearing her voice, I used to miss how she said my name, I used to miss how she walked, I used to miss how she complained about life not being fair and stuff like that. I think that's the most heartbroken I had ever been in my life over a girl, and I think it's because it seemed like things ended before they had even really and truly began. But, it was what it was, sometimes things just end just like that, and we just have to learn to move on, that's part of life, it involves hearts being broken.

It's funny how the universe works though, because at the time when I was going through my heartbreak, there was a cute and lovely young lady staying at my dad's house for the summer. She had just come from Africa and was staying at my dad's house waiting for the fall to go to school (University). I remember when I got out the military and went back to live with my dad (he had moved from D.C. to Maryland) so I could figure out what my next move in life would be after the military, I remember walking into the house and seeing this cute young lady sitting on a couch looking very lovely. I remember asking my sister "who is that?". My sister told me that she's a friend of the family and that she had come from Africa to go to University in the fall. I was like "oh okay, cool". I went and said hi to her and she looked at me and softly said hi back. She seemed kinda shy, and I really didn't bother her much after that, because my focus was still with the Texas girl that I had fallen for and was trying to get her to come visit me. But as time went on me and the cute young lady at the house started becoming very friendly, we started talking a lot and she would reassure me that my heartbreak would go away and that I would be fine. I remember we did a lot of talking and we actually started confiding in each other. I remember her telling me about the loser boys that tried to date her in the past and how she wasn't interested in just casual dating, she wanted serious dating, the kind that could lead into marriage. I remember I used to sit there with her at the house and just listen to her talk and I used to think to myself, wow, what a special lady, and thinking that whoever ends up being with her is gonna be a very lucky guy.

We had a lot of fun, me and the cute young lady that summer, because neither one of us had much to do. I had just got out of the military and I wasn't working or doing anything just yet. And she didn't really have anything to do either, she was just there waiting for her dad to come and take her to University after the summer. So we found ourselves a lot of the time just hanging around the house just chilling. One day we were so bored just sitting around, so I asked her if she wanted to go to the movies, she said sure and we went. I enjoyed hanging out with her, she was very sweet and lovely. We actually ended up going to the movies almost every week, and other times we would just go out to eat. We had fun hanging out and it was pressure free because we actually were just friends, so there was no pressure of trying to impress each other (like if it was a date and the thought of romance was in our minds) or anything like that, we could just be ourselves and enjoy hanging out.

But then one day as we went out to eat (Popeyes) something happened. She got up to go get a refill on her drink and asked me if I wanted a refill as well. I said yes and she took my cup and walked to get the refills. I watched her as she walked and then my heart skipped a beat, and I said to myself, oh no heart, don't do this to me, I'm not ready to be catching feelings at the moment, I'm still not really over the broken heart that I had just gone through not that long ago. But my heart wouldn't leave me alone, it kept skipping a beat. When she came back with the refills and sat back down I just looked at her and thought, oh no, this can't be happening to me again, not so soon. But, I kept my cool and we just kept chilling as friends. Then the summer came to an end and it was time for her to leave for school. I remember I started missing her already, even before she had left. And then the day came that her father was coming to pick her up and take her to the University, somewhere in Pennsylvania. I remember I spent the whole day just looking at her and wishing she didn't have to leave or wishing the University was closer. But she had to go and I prepared myself to say bye to her. But, I had a cousin who had come from London to visit and he wanted me to drive him to Virginia to see a friend that he hadn't seen in years. The friend used to live and go to school with him in London, but she had moved to the U.S. years back and they hadn't seen each other in a long time. I kept telling him no, not today, maybe tomorrow, because I wanted to be there and say bye to the girl before she left. But he kept begging me saying her dad is not coming till the evening and we'll be back long before her dad gets here. I finally gave up and I agreed to drive him to his friend, which was about 45 minutes away. When we got there he and his friend just kept on talking and talking and talking and I just kept looking at the time which was flying by. I finally told him we had to go because it was already about 4:30pm and her dad was supposed to come around 5 or 6pm. So he said his good bye to his friend and we rushed out of there and jumped into the car and I drove like a mad man trying to get back to the house to catch the girl before she left. But when we got to the house she was gone, her dad had already come to pick her up and she was gone. I remember feeling very bad, I couldn't believe I missed saying bye to her. My cousin kept apologizing for making me late and missing saying goodbye to the girl, but I was very unhappy, I had a huge bout of sadness in me, I remember holding back tears. I remember my little cousin (who had also come from London to visit) came downstairs to where I was and put her hand on my shoulder and asked me in her British accent she said "are you okay", "are you crying", "you really liked her did you", "you really miss her", "don't cry, it's gonna be okay". I guess she was trying to comfort me, but her saying those words just made me even more emotional, I had to work real hard to fight back the tears.

The next day the girl called to say she got there ok and all is well. I got a chance to talk to her and I apologized for not being there to say goodbye and she said she actually felt bad leaving without saying goodbye to me. Then I got the phone number to her room and told her that I was gonna go see her in about two weeks. After that day she called and I got her number, I ended up calling her everyday, sometimes twice a day (early in the morning to wake her up for her classes and in the evening to say goodnight). I remember missing her a lot and telling her that I was gonna go see her soon. She didn't really believe that I was gonna drive all the way to Pennsylvania to see her, it was about three hours away. So the weekend that I told her I was gonna go see her had come. I had to work that morning (8-12pm, it was a Sunday) and then after work I was gonna drive straight to her University in Pennsylvania. I remember that day at work I was very anxious and my mind was not on my job at all (I did security at the time). I couldn't stop thinking about why I was really going to see her, you know, was it just a friendly visit or was it a visit for me to reveal to her how I really felt about her and maybe we could start a serious relationship. I kid you not, I literally spent the whole four hours of my work shift trying to decide whether my visit is just as a friend or did I want to be with her in a much serious way. I'm talking marriage type seriousness, because I just had a feeling that if I told her that I really liked her and that I think we should be together and if she really liked me also, I had a feeling we were gonna end up married sooner than later, because that's the type of relationship that she was interested in, you know, the relationship that could lead to marriage. So I spent the whole shift trying to figure out if I was ready for a relationship that could lead to marriage, because that's how serious I knew I had to be if I wanted to be with her.

So I spent the whole shift just pacing back and forth, and walking around the building complex none stop (usually I would sit for a long while and then walk around a little bit making my rounds, but this day I did not sit down even once) just thinking, thinking, and more thinking, just examining myself to see if I think I could handle that kind of relationship, because I did not want to mess with her and then disappoint her and break her heart, if I wasn't serious enough to go all the way through to marriage if we started dating. Also, I knew that she wasn't into just shacking up, so if I really wanted to be with her, marriage would have to be in the near horizon sooner than later. I knew all this from all the numerous talks that we had when we were just friends hanging out, that she wanted someone serious, not just casual dating. So after my shift ended, I changed my clothes from the security officer ones to my regular clothes and jumped in my car and headed to Pennsylvania to her University to go see her. On my way there I kept thinking, okay, I'll make my decision on whether to reveal my feelings to her and tell her that I think we should be together based on how my heart reacts when I see her. If my heart jumps with extreme joy when I see her then I will reveal my feelings to her and tell her that I think we should be together, but if my heart jumps with just regular average joy I will not reveal my feelings to her and we can just continue as just friends. Because up to that point I was still not really sure if I was truly ready for a serious relationship commitment, the type that I knew she required.

The drive to her University was kinda long, I remember driving through mountains, valleys and all kinds of terrains, but I eventually got there. When I got there, I parked my car and walked to her dorm building and called her from a pay phone that was outside the building (this was way before cell phones) and told her I had arrived. A few minutes later she came bursting through the door half running and came and gave me the biggest hug ever. She couldn't believe that I had actually come all the way there to her University to see her. She seemed so happy to see me, and I was definitely happy to see her. She looked very pretty and my heart was very overjoyed to see her again. We spent the day going to the movies, going to eat and just hanging out and talking. I remember that whole time I was thinking to myself "yes, I think she's the one, if I'm ever going to get married, I think she's the one that I wouldn't mind being married to". And I was thinking all this before I even really knew how she really felt about me, you know, whether she just liked me as a friend and or if she really liked me for a serious relationship. So as the day drew to a close and I had to leave (because I actually had classes early the next morning, I had enrolled in college that fall, P.G. College), I kept trying to master the courage to tell her that I really liked her and that I think we should be together. But I was so nervous, I remember my heart was beating real fast. I remember I was sitting on a bench and she was standing right next to me real close, and she said it was getting late, I should go ahead and start driving back because I had class early the next day. But I was not ready to go, I did not want to leave, I was enjoying being there with her. But she said she didn't want me driving back so late at night and that I could come back the following weekend to see her again. So I said okay and I got up and reached for her hand and looked at her and told her that I think we should be together. She looked at me for a few seconds and asked me what did I mean by be together. I told her that I mean together together, you know, in a serious way. She looked at me and asked "are you sure?" And I said yes. I don't really remember what she said after that, I'm drawing a blank in my head, lol. All I remember is her telling me that it's getting late and I should start getting back. Then I said okay and pulled her closer to me and asked her if I could give her a goodbye kiss. She thought about it for a few seconds and said okay, just a small one. Then we kissed for a little bit, I wanted to kiss her some more but she pulled away and said I had to go. So we then hugged and then I walked to my car and drove back to Maryland. I really don't remember much of my drive back to Maryland, because I was pretty much in a dream zone, just thinking about how great it was hanging out with her and how we actually kissed. I was on cloud nine!

The following weekend I did go see her again, I don't really remember much from that weekend besides me just wanting to hug her and hold her hand all the time. I do remember I did have a car issue, I think my car was overheating and or dripping oil, something like that and I remember we tried to find a mechanic shop but they all seemed to be closed, it was a small town in Pennsylvania. We had fun hanging out that day, a lot of hand holding, hugging, and a bit more kissing, which was fantastic and I knew she was definitely the one for me, and I really wanted her in my life.

I continued to call her everyday, sometimes twice a day. Then fast forward about three months later, I called her one day and she sounded very distraught. I asked her what's going on and she said that the financial aid office told her that her financial aid has some serious issues and that she is in danger of not being able to attend classes the next semester, which meant she would have to leave the school. I remember she was thinking maybe she should just return to Africa or perhaps go to London where her older sister lived. I started panicking, I couldn't believe I may lose the chance to be with her. I did some quick thinking and told her "no, don't go back to Africa and don't go to London, just come back to Maryland and stay with me and we'll figure out the rest together". Then she asked me "stay with you where?" At that time I was still staying at my dad's house. So I told her I'm gonna get a place and we can move in together. She was very hesitant of the idea of moving in with me, she was really leaning towards moving to London. I told her trust me, we can make it work, just take a chance with me, we can do this together. I told her I can go pick her up after the current semester is over and she'll just have to stay at my dad's house for a short period (while I look for a place), then we can move in together. She really did not want to do the shacking up thing. So I told her not to worry, we're gonna get married as soon as we move in together, so we won't be shacking up for long at all. She said she'll think about it, and we hung up the phone.

A few days later as we spoke she said okay she'll move in with me, I just have to make sure that she won't be staying at my dad's house for long and that we won't be shacking up for long. I was so happy she said okay and I increased my work hours at my job so I can have a better pay stub to start searching for an apartment. After the semester was over (towards the end of December) I went to pick her up. She seemed kinda uneasy but she was happy to see me. We drove back to Maryland ready to take on our new adventure of figuring out life together. I wasted no time and went down to D.C. Courthouse to apply for a marriage license. I filled out the form and signed it and then I took it to the house and gave it to my lovely lady to sign it. She stared at the form for a few seconds and asked me if I was sure I wanted to go through with the marriage. I said yes I'm very sure. She then signed her part and the next day I took the form back to the Courthouse and they gave us a February date for the marriage. I went back and told my lovely lady that we are set for February and she seemed excited about it. But finding a decent and affordable apartment proved to be a little bit of a challenge, as the February date got near we still hadn't found an apartment yet. So I decided to cancel the February date because I didn't want us getting married while still living at my dad's house. So I told her that we are gonna have to temporarily postpone the marriage until we move out. But she did not take that decision very well, she thought I was changing my mind and was trying to use the temporary postponement as a way out. So I quickly went back to the Courthouse and asked them if I can change the date of the marriage just one month, they said sure and gave us a March date. I then went to my lovely lady and told her that we are now set for March, and she seemed a little bit more assured that we will be getting married soon. Then I realized that my pay stubs were not high enough to rent a decent place so we decided we should just get a roommate to share a decent two bedroom apartment with. So we had a friend lease an apartment with us and we were able to get the apartment in early March.

After we got the apartment and moved in, it was time to get ready for the marriage day, which was only about three weeks away but we still hadn't told anybody about it, not one single person, only me and her knew about it. Then she said we have to start telling people, especially our parents. But, neither one of us was actually comfortable bringing the topic to our parents, because we both knew that they most likely are not going to be in favor of the idea of us getting married just like that, without going through some traditional processes. So I told her, you know what, let's just elope and then we'll tell our parents afterwards. She strongly did not like that idea, so we had to master up some courage and just tell our parents that we're gonna do the Courthouse marriage for now and we'll do the big wedding ceremony later down the road. But we still procrastinated until the final week before the marriage date and that's when we told our parents and other family members. Our parents weren't so sure about the marriage idea, but her mom gave us her blessings and we proceeded with the marriage. Only a few family members were able to make it because for one, it happened on a weekday afternoon (Thursday around 2pm), and for two; we told people so last minute they were not able to schedule their work hours around it. So we had only a few family members to witness it. But the ceremony was nice, sweet and short, and when the judge pronounced us husband and wife, I looked at my lovely wife and said to myself, I can't believe I actually married this lovely lady, I can't believe that I actually became the lucky guy that I said who ever will end up with her will be a lucky guy. Then I kissed my lovely wife and we walked out that Courthouse as a newlywed couple full of love and optimism of a happy marriage. I won't say it has all been rosy, no, there's been some bumps and bruises, but for the most part we have had a good marriage so far and we are still going strong after 23 years of marriage and having raised three wonderful children, blessed be to God.

So, what do you think about my journey to love? Kinda crazy ha! But almost everyone has a crazy journey before they find that one person that will make them say "okay, I think this is the one for me." And the only question that will remain is to ask themselves, should I marry this person or not. And if they do decide to marry the person, then that will mean that they have reached their journey to love. But, if they decide that the person they are in a relationship with is probably not the one, and therefore decide not to marry them, then that will mean that they have not reached their journey to love yet, because they will still be searching and looking for the one that they believe to be the one for them, and then marry them and say "I Do". Okay I hope you enjoyed this chapter, it was a fun but also kinda tough chapter to write, because I had to do a lot of remembering, but it was very enjoyable to reminisce and see how my journey to love actually unfolded. Now let's get into the nitty gritty of marriage, which begins with finding the right person for you, you know, finding Mr. or Mrs. Right!

"I DO"

2

FINDING MR. OR MRS. RIGHT

The most crucial part of trying to ensure that you have a chance for a successful marriage is finding the person that you believe has the qualities that you are looking for in a partner. And by qualities I don't really mean the physical qualities, no, I'm more so speaking of the inner qualities, you know, like, is the person caring, friendly, thoughtful, smart, ambitious, and so on. The inner qualities are the most crucial in giving a marriage a real chance for success. Because I mean, a person can be as handsome or as beautiful as can be, but if their inner self is terrible the chance of a successful marriage will greatly diminish. Now, of course a person's attractiveness is a nice addition to a person's inner quality, as it is usually the initial reason why you were interested in getting to know them better in the first place. But, physical attractiveness can not maintain a marriage if the inner qualities of the partners are not good.

Now, how do you go about finding a partner who has the qualities that you are looking for? Well, that's where dating comes in. But before you can date, you have to find a person to date, and not just any person, but a person you believe may have the qualities you are looking for in a married partner. You may want to ask me "how am I supposed to know if a person seems to have the qualities that I'm looking for before I even go on a first date with them". Well, that's what phone conversations are for, you know, you can talk to the person you are interested in on the phone for a long while if you have to, until you start to get the feeling that the person may have the qualities you may be looking for in a married partner. You see, most people rush through phone conversations, they don't spend enough time asking their potential date enough questions to give them a good insight into the person, they usually just engage in sweet talk as the guy tries to woo the woman into going out with him. But it's a good idea to engage in several good conversations that involve asking key questions that may give you an idea of the person's inner quality before you even go on a first date. Because sometimes if you rush into a first date before getting some answers beforehand, you may find yourself caught up in the person's physical attraction that you end up not paying much attention to the conversation on the date that you may miss asking key questions, like: do they have children, what is their education level, what do they do for a living, what are their dreams and aspirations, and etc. Most often people tend to find themselves falling for someone before they even really know if that person actually has the qualities they are really looking for, like: the person's temperament, the person's spirituality, the person's background, and etc. And some people may even end up marrying someone that they don't really even know that well, but they have so fallen in love with that person that they ignore all the warning signs that shows the person they are thinking of marrying is of low inner quality and that the chances of their marriage working out is zero to none. And this is what is called "Fools Rush In". You can't rush into getting married, you have to really examine if the person you are thinking of marrying really has the potential to be a good marriage partner with you.

So, now that you know what qualities you are looking for in a partner, how do you go about trying to find a person that can match or come close to matching those qualities, because as the saying goes, finding a good man or a good woman is a very big challenge nowadays. And this does not mean that there's not a lot of good men and good women out there, no, it just means it's hard to find them, especially in this age where a lot of casual dating seem to be taking place, you know, where people seem to be more into sleeping around than being serious about getting into a committed relationship, which is what a marriage is. Most people are actually scared of getting married, especially guys. And this is because most guys just don't like the idea of being tied down, you know, settling down with just one woman. And this is because guys are naturally hunters by nature, and they like to hunt new prey every once in a while, you know what I mean? So settling down for guys is not really an easy thing, because they know they will have to go against their nature, which most guys fear doing. But, if a guy finds a woman that he thinks is very special, he will be willing to give up his hunting nature and accept settling down with that one woman.

Now, let's explore how a person can make themselves available in order to have the potential to meet these good men and good women that are out there. One of the best ways is to make sure you are not doing casual dating, meaning you are not just dating for dating's sake, you know, you not just having fun dating without trying to find Mr. or Mrs. Right. Which means you won't just be going out on dates with different people just to waste time, just because you are bored or because you are so sexy that people are throwing themselves at you and you can't resist but accept the dates. That is a waste of time, especially if you are serious about finding Mr. or Mrs. Right, you just can't do casual dating, your dating has to be more serious, the type of serious where you want to meet the person's family and friends. That's one of the best ways to know if the person you are dating is serious about you or not, because a person who is not serious will seldom want to introduce you to their families, because they understand by introducing you to their family it means the relationship is becoming serious. That's why you don't want to just do casual dating, because you will almost never get to meet the person's family, because your date does not see you as a long term potential partner, which means instead of them seeing you as a potential Mr. or Mrs. Right, they mostly just see you as a Mr. or Mrs. Right Now. So not doing casual dating makes you available to have the potential to meet the special person when they present themselves to you, because you won't be occupied with just chasing dates, but you will be more focused on waiting for that special someone to present themselves into your life, as you will be dating people who seem to be more willing to be in a serious relationship. And how do you know if they are serious, it's by them taking you to meet their families.

Now, another way a person can make themselves available in order to have the potential to meet these good men and women that are out there is by not dating a loser and or getting into a relationship with a loser. And what I mean by a loser is, dating someone whom you know has no business actually being with you, you know, someone who does not deserve you, you know, someone who does not appreciate and or don't even seem to care much about you, you know, someone who just seems to just be taking, taking, taking from you without reciprocating your kindness towards them, you know, someone who just seems to drain you, instead of uplifting you. A lot of people get caught up, they just find themselves fallen for the wrong person but find it very hard to break up with that person, thereby they end up dragging the doomed relationship longer than it needs to be dragged and inadvertently make themselves unavailable to potentially meet the right person for them, even if the person is staring them right in their face, they just pass up the opportunity because they are still dragging a doomed relationship. A lot of times people stay in doomed relationships because they have children together, therefore they prolong the relationship because of the children, even though the relationship is pretty much done, they have just not said it to each other yet. Why stay in a doomed relationship when you are not married to the person, what's the point in that? Why not just call it quits and cut your losses and free yourself and make yourself available to potentially meet Mr. or Mrs. Right? But a lot of people prolong toxic relationships when their Mr. or Mrs. Right could be right around the corner waiting on them to be available.

Another way for a person to make themselves available in order to have the potential to meet some of these good men and women that are out there is by not having children out of wedlock, you know, not having kids before you are married, especially for women. Why do I say especially for women, it's because even a good man can be chased away by a good woman who has kids, especially if the guy has no kids. And this is because guys who have no children usually don't want the responsibility of raising other guy's kids, thereby they can get scared away by the thought of being step daddy. So it's very important for women to try their best not to have children before they are married, otherwise they will find it harder to find Mr. Right, especially if they have more than one child, the more the children the harder it gets. Women tend to be a little bit more open to marrying a guy who has children, and it's because usually the children will be in the custody of their mother, you know, the children would be living full time with their mother and the guy would just have them for the weekend or on holidays, so the potential Mrs. Right won't regard the guy's children as a deal breaker in marrying the guy, because she won't have to deal with the other woman's children that much. It's not fair, but usually when couples break up, the woman tends to be left with the children, while the guy just makes visitations, and sometime (probably more often than not) the guy (the father of the children) becomes an absent father and the woman ends up having to raise the children on her own. So women should be extra picky on whom they have a baby with, or just wait until they find their Mr. Right and then have as many babies as they want with him, lol.

Now, let's talk about where these good men and good women can be found at, because everybody swears that finding a good man and or a good woman is hard nowadays. And some even swear that there's no more good men or women out there, but I disagree. The reason why I disagree is because millions of couples get married each year around the world, and I don't believe all of them are not good men or women. And even as the statistic says, that half of all marriages end in divorce, even that being so, it doesn't mean there's no more good men or women out there, no, it just means that a lot of people marry the wrong people. And since half of all marriages seem to survive (at least for the first ten years), it means that there are millions of good men and women out there, it's just that you have to try your best to pick the right partner so y'all can be the half that makes it, the half that stays together, happily. So there are a lot of good men and good women out there (probably more good women than men, which can make it a little bit more of a challenge for women to find the right person for them), it just takes a little bit more work to find them, and this is where it becomes crucial to try and make sure you date someone who is not just attractive, but someone who displays the inner qualities that you want in a marriage partner.

So, where can these good men and women be hiding at? They are actually not hiding at all, they are everywhere, you just have to learn how to recognize them. One of the best ways to start the recognition is from what they talk about in your conversation with them, you can discern a lot about a person from what they seem to like to talk about more often than not. Also, a person's personality will manifest itself through conversation, you know, you will be able to tell if the person seems smart, or if they have a sense of humor, or if they are straight forward, or if they seem to just want to play games, and etc. And also for ladies, you will be able to gauge if the person seem genuine in really wanting to know you from how they first approach you (most often than not), and you can use your God given sixth sense to sniff them out, you know, the gut feeling that you get from when they first approach you, trust that gut feeling, no matter how handsome the guy is, always trust your gut feeling. But good men and women are all around you, you just have to give them a chance to showcase themselves. And how do you give them a chance to showcase themselves, it's by asking them a lot of important questions about themselves, even before you agree to go on a first date with them, because you don't want to find yourself hypnotized by their sexiness and or handsomeness that you forget all about the important questions you had planned on asking them on the date, all because you couldn't get enough of staring at their cuteness, lol.

It takes a lot of focus and discipline for a woman to not allow herself to fall for a guy's charm and handsomeness and forget to really examine the guy. This is how a lot of ladies tend to have children with guy's whom they deep down know are not really the right person for them, but the guy's charm and cuteness made them lose focus and end up letting the guy impregnate them, and then they are surprised that the guy dumps them not long after the baby is born. Guys too tend to fall for a lady's sexiness and cuteness that they lose focus and allow themselves to impregnate the lady and then get surprised that the lady is not really the right person for them and therefore ends up dumping her not long after the baby is born. Both sides take the blame for not being as careful in choosing a partner as they should be. And so if you don't want to be one of those people who have children by the wrong person, waiting until you are married to have children is usually the best way to help you focus and discipline yourself to not allow just any guy to be the father of your children, and for guys to not allow just any woman to be the mother of their children.

So, it's really a very tricky situation how you discover your Mr. Right or Mrs. Right, because you can't just tell off the bat, you know, you will have to actually do some serious examination of the person before you can feel very confident the person you are dating is the right person for you. But you will eventually know, because you will start to say to yourself things like: wow, it's amazing how caring this person is, or, wow, it's amazing how wonderful this person is, or, it's amazing how sweet this person is, or, it's amazing how responsible this person is, or, it's amazing how much of a hard worker this person is, and so on and so on, the person will just start to leave you with amazement at how good their inner self really is, and you will start to think to yourself, you know what, maybe this is the one. And that's when you will ask yourself that very important question, which is: should I marry this person or not. If you decide to marry the person then most likely than not you have found your Mr. or Mrs. Right. But if you decide not to marry the person then most likely you have not found your Mr. or Mrs Right, or maybe you are just way too picky to recognize a good man or a good woman when they are right there staring you at your face, showing you that they have the inner qualities to be a good marriage partner to you. But usually your instincts are right, there may be something about the person you're dating that you just don't think you will be able to overlook or you don't think the person will be able to change whatever their shortcomings and or bad habits are that kinda makes you feel uneasy about marrying them. I always say follow your gut instincts, because sometimes you may be dating an overall nice and caring person but they may have some habits that can kinda really get in your nerves and they don't see their habits as a problem, but to you it's kind of a big deal. Now, of course no one is perfect, we all have our little flaws and or little habits here and there, but you will have to determine if those little habits and or flaws that the person you are dating has is a deal breaker or not, no matter how small they may seem to the outside world, or to your family and friends. Because at the end of the day, you are the one that is gonna have to live in the same household with the person, and so if those supposedly small habits of theirs keeps popping up, you can easily find yourselves arguing all the time, with him or her saying you are making a big deal out of nothing, and you saying you promised you would stop. And then he or she may say you found me and married me with my little habits, so why are you making it a big deal of them now. To which you will really not have much of a comeback to that, because they are right, you did meet them and married them with their little habits (which can turn big over time), so why is it a big issue now, after y'all are married. Because marrying someone it actually means you are accepting that person with whatever flaws and or habits they come with. So it's up to you to decide how many flaws and or habits you are willing to tolerate from your Mr. and or Mrs. Right, because after you say "I Do", those flaws and or habits should not be an issue, because you chose to marry them with their issues that they came with.

So as you can see, there's a lot of examination that you have to do before you decide if the person you are dating may be the one or not, because you don't want too many surprises to pop up about the person you have married that you didn't examine before you married the person, otherwise you will end up asking yourself "who the hell did I marry?", lol. I mean, wouldn't that be terrible, to wake up one morning not long after you got married to them and start thinking and saying to yourself "oh no, I think I made a mistake marrying this person!" I mean, how terrible would that be? That would be extremely terrible, right? Because not only will you have married the wrong person (not Mr. or Mrs. Right), and not only have you spent thousands of dollars on a big wedding marrying the wrong person, but you will have to endure uneasiness in your marriage, which will mean you won't be in a happy marriage, which will mean divorce will be coming sooner than later. And this is how a lot of people end up divorcing not long after they are married, and it's because they didn't really take their time to really examine the person they are dating and ended up marrying a stranger, so to speak. Now, some people do get fooled by the people they are dating to think that they are dating the most wonderful person on the earth, but then that person can switch on them and turn out to be really the opposite than what they showcased of themselves while dating. You know, while dating they seem to be so caring and sweet, but then after getting married they showcase their real true colors, as they start becoming very mean and or uncaring to their partner. And you will be left there thinking to yourself, what the hell just happened, who did I really marry, I can't believe they deceived me of their true selves. If this happens to you, divorce them with the quickness, go get an annulment if possible (I think you can if it's within just a few short months of marriage), don't allow yourself to go through the misery of trying to make it work, no, they deceived you pretending to be sweet but they were actually ugly inside, you don't need all that ugly and misery in your life, no, life is too short and too precious to waste it on someone who doesn't cherish you, especially if you don't have any children with them yet, there's no need to try to make it work, just cut your losses and make yourself available for the real Mr. or Mrs. Right to present themselves to you, so you can marry the right person for you.

Well okay, I think I have shared enough about how to go about finding Mr. and or Mrs. Right, as I dealt mostly with examining the inner qualities of the person whom you are dating, as that is more crucial than the outside appearance of the person, because the outside appearance will start to kinda fade a little bit over time, you know, as the person gets older and their body and face starts sagging and all that kind of stuff, lol. And of course yes we all want and or desire attractive people to be in a relationship with, but as the saying goes, beauty is indeed in the eyes of the beholder. Because a person with a beautiful inner self will start to radiate that inner beauty on their outside appearance as the person they are dating gets to know them better and the person who is dating them will start to see them as being beautiful both in the inside and outside, no matter how average looking they may appear to the rest of the world, but to the person who knows them best, they will be above average looking in their eyes. So don't get so caught up on the outside beauty of a person first all the time and not give the so called average looking people a chance to get to know them better, because your Mr. or Mrs. Right may be the man or woman that appears to be average looking to the outside world, but may turn out to actually be above average looking once you get to know them better and once their inside beauty starts to shine, and you start to recognize that they are actually good looking, even if you are the only one that sees it. So don't be afraid to give an average looking person a chance to showcase their inner beauty to you, because you may just be surprised at how wonderful they are, and you can end up falling in love with them, because as the saying goes, "beauty is only skin deep!"

Okay, I hope I have shared enough about finding Mr. or Mrs. Right. Now let's move on to the next chapter, which deals with perhaps the most important part of a couple's relationship, which is: the wedding day!!!

3

THE WEDDING DAY

The Wedding Day is perhaps the most important day in a couple's relationship, because this is the day that the two become as one (as the Bible says), as they go from living their lives as two individual persons to joining their lives and living together as one unit, as husband and wife, after they say "I Do". The wedding day is very special, as it's the day that the couple give each other the ultimate of commitment to each other, as they pledge to forsake all others and be with each other till death do them apart. What an awesome and serious commitment that is, isn't it? I mean, think about it for a second, you are telling your partner that you want to be with them for the rest of your life, no matter what, whether the two of you become rich or poor (most marriages struggle tremendously when the couple becomes poor), or if one or both of you become sick, or if the two of you go through good times or bad times, no matter what, you want to always be there with that person, no matter what. Isn't that fantastic and kinda scary at the same time? Why scary, you may ask? Because, what if the two of you end up not working out, you know, the two of you end up not learning how to be married to each other and end up just fighting all the time and driving each other crazy, wouldn't that really suck, especially after all that promise to love and to be with each other forever no matter what (as the marriage vows say).

And this is why the wedding day is the most important day in a couple's relationship, because the two of you are giving each other the utmost of commitment to each other, you are telling each other

53

that I want to be by your side and go through this life journey together, no matter what. I mean, how awesome is that!? I can't think of any other kinds of commitments that two people can make to each other that can match that of a marriage commitment, can you? And this is why marriage is a serious business, not one that should be entered into lightly, you know, without extra precaution. Because you don't want to be one of those people that finds themselves trapped in a terrible marriage and therefore will have to make the most painful decision to end the marriage, which will mean you will be breaking your commitment to the other person whom you said you will love and be with forever, no matter what. But as we all know, marriage is not an easy institution, it takes two very committed and willing partners to work at making it work, one partner can't make a marriage work by themselves, no matter how hard they try, both partners have to be willing to work at it, especially if they truly love each other.

And this is why the wedding day is very special, because it's the day that the couple prove to each other how much they really love and care for each other, by giving each other the ultimate commitment to love and care for each other for the rest of their lives. Isn't that so special, having someone you really love show you how much they too really love you by giving you the ultimate commitment that they want to be with you forever. Isn't that so wonderfully special! And this is why most couples tend to cry on their wedding day, and it's because they get overwhelmed by the joy of realizing that they are actually about to marry the person they have fallen in love with, the person that they want to be with for the rest of their lives. There's no joy like the one of hearing the person you are in love with say the words "I Do". These two words are so magical, as they demonstrate the ultimate commitment of love for the couple.

Now, before the couple can say "I Do" to each other, there's some preparations to do, you know, to make preparations for the wedding day. And before the couple can start on the preparation for the wedding, there's an engagement period and process that needs to take place. And before the engagement period and process can take place, there's a proposal that needs to take place, which is usually the responsibility of the man, you know, the man needs to ask the woman for her hand in marriage, you know, the man needs to ask the woman if she will marry him. It's amazing the amount of responsibility and or power the man has in deciding whether the couple will take their relationship to the ultimate level (marriage) or not, and the woman has no choice but to wait for her man to make the decision. And a lot of men tend to take their time in making this decision, whether consciously or not. And some men never seem to be ready and or able to make the decision, which tends to lead their women to keep nagging them about whether or not they're gonna ask them to get married or not. But some men are just so scared of marriage that they will risk losing a good woman by keeping delaying the asking until the woman gives up on them and leaves them. Then the man is surprised that she actually left him, then he tries to get her back by proposing to her, but by this point she doesn't really trust that his proposal is genuine and ends up turning him down and moves on to find her true Mr. Right who won't take too long to recognize her specialness and pop the big question.

But, yeah, the decision for the couple to get married or not pretty much belongs to the guy, as he has to do the proposing, otherwise the couple's relationship will be stuck on the girlfriend and boyfriend stage forever, or until the woman manages to get the guy to realize that he may lose her if he doesn't propose soon. And this is why it's important for the women to let the men they are dating know that they expect the relationship to lead to something serious, as serious as marriage sooner than later, because otherwise the guy will just place house as long as he can without popping the big question for marriage. But if a guy knows that the woman he is dating is not interested in just a boyfriend and girlfriend relationship but wants marriage to be in the timeline sooner than later, he will start preparing mentally for the possibility of them getting married soon, and will start planning how he is going to do the proposal.

The proposal is what most women in a relationship look forward to, as it signals that it is time to start planning the wedding that they have been dreaming of since they were little girls. Am I right or wrong? I believe am right, because almost all girls have dreamed of having a fairytale wedding, you know, a big lavish wedding where they are wearing the most beautiful wedding dress as they come down the aisle looking oh so gorgeous, as their oh so handsome soon to be husband waits for them by the altar to take their hand and say their "I Do's". Am I right or wrong? I believe I am right, because people still spend so much money on weddings, with all that flowers, the limos, the extravagant wedding dresses, the big reception hall with all that decorations and stuff, just so the brides can have their dream weddings, or come close to it. But I understand, I know why ladies want a nice beautiful wedding, it's because it's a very special and emotional day for them, as this is the day they have been dreaming of since they were little girls, and they want to feel special on their wedding day, the day they are getting married to their Mr. Right, aka their Prince Charming, aka the person they are in love with, aka the person who is about to make them a wife, aka the person who is about to become their husband, aka the person they are about to say "I Do" to. So this day is very special to the ladies, as they understand the magnitude of the occasion, and they want the day to feel as magical as the institution of marriage itself is (if it's working the right way, lol).

Now, you may want to ask me, are wedding days not a big deal to guys as it is to the ladies? And the short answer is: it is a big deal as it is for the ladies, but guys (most guys) don't have fairytale dreams about their wedding day, you know what I mean? And what I mean is, most guys don't think and or dream about how big or wonderful their wedding day is going to be, no, most guys when they were younger dreamed about how they gonna be ladies men when they grow up, you know, they dream about being players, you know, dating multiple women, lol. And so for most men the wedding day pretty much doesn't exist until after they propose, but before that, they don't really think about it, they actually think about how not to get caught up and end up in one of their own, lol. So the wedding day is really for the ladies, because most women tend to actually know what kind of wedding they want even before their men propose to them. And actually most women tend to know what kind of wedding they want even before they even have a boyfriend, you know, before they are even dating anyone, you know what I mean? So the wedding day is much more a bigger deal for the ladies than the guys, because the ladies want to feel extra special and beautiful on a day that marks the beginning of her being a married woman and not just a girlfriend, a day she had been looking forward to since she was little.

So now, after the man proposes to his girlfriend, they now enter the engagement stage, in which they become fiancees. And this is the stage where the woman goes around showing off her engagement ring and let's everyone know that she's about to go from being girlfriend to wife soon. And this is the stage where the couple starts planning the wedding. And this is the stage where the couple starts going through pre-marital counseling and in some countries (especially African countries) they start going through traditional pre-marital counseling as well. In the traditional pre-marital counseling, the village elders and or the uncles and aunties start teaching the couple (separately) the traditional duties of the wife and the husband in a marriage, and the things the wife needs to do to best take care of the household and her husband, and the things the husband needs to do to best take care of the household and his wife. I actually got a chance recently (about 3 weeks ago, as I'm writing this book) to sit in on the last session where the bride and groom (who is my brother in law, and me and my wife and kids flew to Africa to be a part of the wedding) were brought to a room together with their teachers and elders and they had to explain all that they were taught in those separate sessions. It was very interesting, I was not ready for it, because they went in, no hold bars, they taught them not only household responsibilities, but also sexual responsibilities to one another, and each had to explain what they were taught about sex and how the marriage bed is not defiled (as the Bible says). And they went in, I kid you not, I almost felt like I was intruding into their married bed. But I guess they had to keep it real, because sex is one of the things that can really hinder a marriage from being good, you know, if the couple neglects to inject intimacy into their marriage on a regular basis.

That was a very interesting session to sit in, I actually learned a lot, and afterwards I told my wife that I think we need to go through the traditional pre-marital counseling, even though we have been married for 23 years already. My wife just looked at me and said no, too late, lol. But I enjoyed sitting in on the session, and you can tell it was serious business, as the bride and groom took turns explaining their roles and or duties as husband and wife traditionally. And the other interesting thing was that, the groom's side (which included me) had to give money to the bride's side every time the bride explained any part of what she was taught about taking care of the household and her husband. I kid you not, every time she finished explaining something, the ladies on her side (her teachers and elders) would demand money to be paid before she continued to explain something else. I kid you not, and the payment amount was not set, no, the payment for each explanation was negotiated at the spot, and after each explanation and before she could do the next explanation the groom's side (which included me) had to hand over some money. I thought the whole thing was madness, because the groom side had to put down how much we thought the explanation was worth and the ladies would either accept the amount or ask for more if they thought the explanation was worth more than what the groom side offered. It was crazy, and I wasn't prepared, I had no cash on me, so

I couldn't help much, and the ladies would look at me at times and say that they accept dollars also. I mean it was insane, the groom's side kept going into their pockets and search for whatever money they had and offering it, but the bride's side kept saying not enough. I wish I had known that I was going to be a part of the session earlier, because I would have gone down there with pockets full of one dollar bills and made it rain on the bride's side every time they asked for more money, lol. But it was serious business for the grooms side to keep offering those money after the bride explained something, because otherwise the ladies (the brides teachers and elders) could stop the bride from continuing to explain, which would mean that the wedding is off, as in, the wedding can not proceed, because the last session would not have been completed. So the groom had no choice but to keep shelling out money to the bride's side, otherwise they couldn't have the bride, because apparently after the last session is complete, the bride actually belongs to the groom, even before they exchange the vowels on their wedding day, because in the eyes of the elders the couple will have completed the process of courting each other and the bride is actually handed over to the groom after the last session, meaning they are now husband and wife traditionally, the wedding is just a formality for the church and the state.

And so, yes, marriage is a serious business, and it's a good idea for the couple to go through pre-marital counseling before they get married. Because for one, it will give the couple a realistic view of what joining together as one actually entails and how to go about preparing themselves for it. And for two, pre-marital counseling will and or help expose any major issues that may exist between the couple that may end up being a big obstacle for the couple to deal with in their marriage, that can affect the joy of their union. Some of these issues can be for instance like; financial (where one or both of the couples may be dealing with financial hardships, like big debts), or spiritual (where the couple belong in two different religions, or one is religious and the other is not), or parenting (where the couple is dealing with baby daddy and or baby mama dramas), or etc. These are some of the obstacles that the couple has to seriously take into account before they get married to each other, because otherwise they can easily find themselves spending so much time arguing over some of these things instead of enjoying their union. And so pre-marital counseling is very important, because it forces the couple to explore any issues that they may have in their relationship and address it in front of a marriage counselor and allow the counselor to help them find a resolution of how they will deal with their issues in a productive way. Also, the pre-marital counseling can help the couple realize that maybe they are not really ready for marriage, as their issues may be a lot bigger than they thought. And in this case, the couple can decide whether to prolong the engagement period and or to postpone the marriage until they have dealt with their issues and are in one accord.

Now, after the couple has gone through the pre-marital counseling and the counselor is satisfied that the couple is well prepared and understands the importance of a marriage union, this is when the couple can start counting down the days till their wedding day, as they begin the process of making final wedding day arrangements. And these final wedding day arrangements can be both exciting and stressful at the same time. And why do I say this, because there's so much that goes into wedding planning and it seems like the last final days before the wedding a lot of arrangement issues seem to pop up, like; the brides dress is not ready yet, or the limos haven't been booked yet, or the food catering hasn't been settled yet, or the bridesmaids dresses don't fit, or the reception hall is too small, or the Dj doesn't know what songs will be played on the day, or not everyone who wanted to come to the wedding has received an invitation, and so on and so on. There's a lot that goes on in planning and arranging a wedding, that's why most couples hire a wedding planner to assist in the planning. And weddings can get very expensive, because there's so much to pay for, that if the couple is not careful they can find themselves spending thousands of dollars on the wedding and end up broke. And ending up broke is not a good way to start a marriage, because the newlyweds can find themselves starting to argue about money issues before even the honeymoon is over, lol. So be extra careful in planning for the wedding, and don't allow peer pressure to force you to have a big expensive wedding if your financial abilities are limited. Work within your means, even if it means going to the courthouse and doing a civil wedding, as me and my wife did.

But weddings are fun, and they are very special, as they mark the beginning of a couple going from boyfriend and girlfriend to husband and wife. And it should be enjoyed to the fullest by the couple and their family and friends, because truth be told, finding that special one that you want to spend the rest of your life with is very special, because as the saying goes, finding a good man or a good woman is hard to do. And as the Bible says, he who finds a wife findeth a good thing, which I can also add that, she who findeth a husband findeth a good thing. So enjoy your wedding day, celebrate the love that you and your partner have found in each other. Celebrate the union that you and your partner have formed. Allow your wedding day to be as magical and special as you feel, for there's nothing like knowing that you have indeed found your Mr. Right or your Mrs. Right. So embrace the moment, for this is the day that the two of you have made the ultimate of commitments to each other, which is to love and care for each other for the rest of your lives.

Now, after the two of you have said your "I Do's", and after the two of you have enjoyed your lavish wedding, and after the two of you have enjoyed your beautiful reception and have danced for the first time as husband and wife, guess what time it is now, yes you guessed it right, it's time for the two of you to get out of there and go to your honeymoon retreat, or to just go home and make love all night long as newlyweds, lol.

4

THE HONEYMOON

The Honeymoon is supposed to be the time that the couple get to know each other more intimately, you know, it is supposed to be the time that the couple get to know each other sexually, you know, it is the time that the couple is supposed to have sex with each other for the first time, you know want I mean? But as we all know, nowadays most couples don't wait till they are married to have sex, no, most couples will have engaged in sex with each other long before marriage. And sometimes the couple not only will have had sex with each other before marriage, but they will have had a child or two before they decide to marry each other. I mean, I don't know what it is, but nowadays people don't seem to put a huge value in waiting till marriage to have sex, you know, like the people in generations past did. Actually, I think it's the over sexualization of society (with casual sex being flaunted all over films, TV, and other medias) that has caused people not to value their virginity as much. You know, it has caused people not to work hard and or not to discipline themselves enough to be able to maintain their virginity until marriage. I mean, there are some people who do try, and some who do succeed to maintain their virginity until marriage, but it's a rarity nowadays. It's even more of a rarity that both partners will have been able to maintain their virginity until they marry each other, usually one of the partners will not be a virgin while the other is. But most often, both partners are not virgins before they marry.

I used to think about maintaining my virginity until I find that special young lady that I wouldn't mind losing my virginity to, you know, the special young lady that I may end up marrying (trying to be a good Christian boy, lol). But one day I was at lunch time in High School and me and this girl that I used to flirt with a little bit kept flirting with me a lot, my friends kept teasing me saying she wants to give me some loving, or something like that. She wasn't really my type like that, and she kind of had a reputation of being kinda loose (promiscuous), which was kind of a turn off for me, as I thought of myself as having higher standards and or being picky. But she told me if I want we could leave after lunch and go to her place, because her mom wouldn't be home. I thought she was playing at first, but after lunch we left and headed home. She lived just about a block or two from where I lived. We ended up going to my apartment building, which had a fitness center in the basement. I went to the receptionist and got the key to the fitness center, then me and the girl went down to the fitness center, we looked around and flirted for a little bit and next thing I knew, I was losing my virginity, lol. Me and the girl messed around a few more times but our entanglement didn't last long, as she quickly realized that she was more into me than I was into her, so our thing didn't last that long at all.

You see how easy it is to lose one's virginity, it can happen just like that, without much thought or effort. And so, this is why it's hard for most people to maintain their virginity till marriage, and it's because the temptation for sexual healing is just too high, you know what I mean? And this is why most couples can't wait until they are married to have sex with each other, and it's because they are around each other all the time, and the temptation for them to engage in some sexual healing with each other becomes very irresistible, especially if they are very flirtatious with each other, you know, very touchy touchy and or kissy kissy. I mean, it's very hard to be very touchy touchy and or kissy kissy with someone and not want to engage sexually with them, especially when the both of you are extremely horny, lol.

And so, anyway, yeah, the honeymoon is supposed to be the first time that the couple get more intimate with each other and enjoy each other sexually. But as we all know, the couple usually has already started enjoying each other sexually before they even thought about being married to each other (casual dating) and so the honeymoon becomes just like another romantic vacation, only this time they will be a married couple. But for those that were able to actually wait till they are married to have sex, the honeymoon becomes even more special, because not only is the couple about to lose their virginity, but they are about to lose their virginity to the person that is actually the love of their life, you know, they are about to lose their virginity to their husband or to their wife. How special is that, isn't that very special? I mean, think about it, you have managed to maintain your sexual purity by maintaining your virginity till marriage and there you are, on your honeymoon, ready to give your sexual purity to not just someone you love, but to someone who is the love of your life, to someone whom you have just married, someone who has vowed to love you for the rest of your life, how sweet is that!? That has to be really sweet to know that you are giving your sexual purity to someone who really loves you and whom you really love, isn't it!? And wouldn't it be even more sweet if both partners are actually virgins on their honeymoon, and are about to share their sexual purity with each other, wouldn't that be so extra sweet!? And this is what the honeymoon was supposed to be all about, you know, for the couple to lose their virginity to each other as they bless their marriage sexually.

But, it is what it is, right!? No one is really worried about whether their partner is a virgin or not before they marry them, right? Most people just hope that they end up with a partner that at least hasn't had any kids yet, right? Am I right or wrong? Isn't that the hope nowadays, that you marry someone that doesn't already have any children? Isn't that pretty much the hope and or wish nowadays? Because truth be told, the chances of you finding and marrying a person that is still a virgin is very unlikely, especially a man. Men just can't do it (most men anyway), it's almost impossible, you know, unless they get married young, you know, like in their late teens or early twenties, but otherwise forget it. And this is because men have too much testosterone which causes them to want to hunt for sexual healing even when they are not that horny. So imagine how much more the urge for a guy to want to hunt for sexual healing when he is horny or better yet, when he is extremely horny. And this is why teenage boys tend to have a hard time taming their hormonal rage and are willing to get sexual healing from any girl that says "hi" to them. And this is why a lot of guys tend to have had a bunch of sexual partners before they get married, and it's because they had a hard time taming their urge to keep hunting for sexual healing. But, there are some guys who are able to tame their sexual urges and not have a lot of sexual partners, but they can be kinda hard to find, especially if they are the type that are regarded as being cute and sexy by society and thereby have women just throw themselves at them and offer up their sex with no effort from the guys. And this is the other reason why it's very hard for guys to maintain their virginity until marriage, and it's because there are just too many women out there that just give up their sex without much effort from the guys, you know, there's just a lot of women out there that just give up their sex so easily, making a guy's chances of losing his virginity so easy.

Now, even though it may be a little bit easier for a woman to try to maintain her virginity till married (because they are usually better at taming their horniness than guys are), a lot of women nowadays tend to not be virgins either before marriage. And I think this is because a lot of women tend to fall for the wrong guys and by the time they realize that they have fallen for the wrong guy it's too late, they have already given up their virginity to the guy, who probably didn't even deserve it. And this is also why a lot of women tend to find themselves being single mothers, and it's because they fell for the wrong guy and ended up giving him children before he has even indicated that marriage will most likely happen between them sooner than later. But, that's life, things happen, and it's so easy to get caught up on someone and end up losing your virginity to the wrong person, instead of losing it to your husband or wife on your honeymoon.

But so anyway, there you are, on your honeymoon, just married, enjoying some romantic time with your husband or wife, feeling very special, feeling very loved, not wanting the honeymoon days to end, but they have to end sometime, you can't be on honeymoon forever, real life of marriage awaits you at home, whether you like it or not, lol. Now, even though the vacationing honeymoon part is over, the couple is really still in the honeymoon phase of their marriage that first year of marriage, as the excitement of being newlyweds still remains for almost the whole first year of marriage, as people continue to wish the couple congratulations on being just married. And also, for that first year the couple will still be excited about seeing each other everyday, you know, excited about waking up in the morning everyday next to their lovely wife or husband. And the couple will still be excited about going out to eat and or just walking around the park hand in hand as husband and wife. And the couple will be excited about joining their bank accounts as a married couple. And the couple will be excited about paying bills together. And the couple will be excited about finally having kids and starting a family as husband and wife. There's just so many things that the newlywed couple will be excited about that first year, because everything is still pretty fresh, and they are excited to work as a unit as husband and wife. But then, the first year will come to a close, and the second year will begin, and the marriage will start to settle and the couple will start to see and realize that not everyday will be roses, as they start to notice that there's some differences in how they think and or like to do things, differences that they kinda let slide in that first year, but are starting to find it hard to ignore and let slide in the second year of marriage, because it kinda starts to annoy them.

And this is where the real marriage life for the couple begins, in the second year of marriage, where the excitement of the newness of the marriage is starting to fade out, and is being replaced by the reality of trying to merge and or navigate how to live together as a unite without letting small issues and or small differences become big issues and or big differences that can interfere with the couple's marriage going as smoothly as possible. And this is the secret on how to have a successful marriage, which is, to learn how to not let small issues and or differences become big issues and or differences, because if you and your spouse don't learn how to deal with the small issues before they become big issues, the chances of your marriage lasting long is very slim to none, because eventually one or both of you will get tired of continuing to fight over and over about small issues that become big issues that you will just find yourself unhappy in the marriage and want to end it. But if you and your spouse can learn how to deal with the small issues before they become big issues, the two of you will have a better chance of having a long lasting marriage.

Now, what are some of these small issues that can turn into big issues, and how can we learn how to deal with them before they turn into big issues? Well, I would love to explore some of these issues with you but I can't do it in this chapter, as this chapter deals with the honeymoon, and issues usually tend to start popping up after the honeymoon period is over. So, why don't we create another chapter in the book called "The Honeymoon is Over ", and use that chapter to explore some of the issues that may start to pop up in the marriage. Is that ok with you? It is!? Oh okay, cool, that is fine with me too, lol. So would you do me an honor and turn to the next chapter of the book, so we can start exploring issues in marriages that can cause problems in the marriage if not dealt with before they become big issues. Thank you very much!

5

THE HONEYMOON IS OVER

So, the Honeymoon is Over, oh oh, looks like marriage troubles are about to start, hopefully not yet, because it's only been one year of marriage, how much trouble can the marriage be in after only one year!? Well my friends, trouble in a marriage can start even within a few months after the Honeymoon. We used to have a neighbor when we stayed at the apartments in Hyattsville, MD. The neighbor was a single dad raising his teenage son. We hardly saw him bring any women home, I think he didn't want to introduce any women to his son whom he knew he wasn't serious about. But then one day we started seeing a woman coming to his place a lot, and we figured he must really be interested in her. To make a story short, one day I saw him wearing a tuxedo, and I said to him "Hey, you looking nice, what's the occasion?" And he said "Hey thank you, I'm actually about to go get married today!" And I said "Hey that's great, congratulations!" And he said "Thank you, I appreciated it!" And off he went to get married. A few days later I saw him and the women packing things from his apartment into a Uhaul truck. He was moving out, and I'm guessing he was moving to her place, as they are married now, and are about to move in together and start their married life. I did not see the guy again until about three or four months later, I ran into him at a Giant Foods store in Hyattsville. We greeted each other with hand shakes, and I asked him how he was doing and how the marriage was going. He said he was doing fine but the marriage was terrible, not only terrible but that the marriage was actually over. Yes, you read that right, his marriage was over already, the marriage did not even last one year, it was over in about 3 or 4 months. I was so surprised, but the look on his face when he said "it was terrible" said it all. He had a disgusted look on his face when he said "it was terrible", then told me that he had already talked to the landlord at our apartment building to see if he can get his old apartment back.

I don't remember asking the guy about what happened to his marriage for it to end so quickly, but I remember thinking to myself, wow, that's the fastest that I have ever heard of a marriage ending. And I also remember thinking to myself, I hope they didn't spend a lot of money on the wedding, you know what I mean?, lol. I mean, can you imagine spending a lot of money on a wedding for it to only last for about three or four months. How terrible would that be? What a waste of your hard earned money that would be, right? So I really hope they didn't spend too much money on their wedding, that would be terrible. But, this is a good example of how a marriage can end very soon if the couple has not learned how to be married to each other. Because I'm suspecting that, for their marriage to have become terrible that quickly, it means that the two of them must not have truly known each other as well as they thought they did. Because for their marriage to end that quickly, it must mean that one or both of the partners were caught off guard with the behavior and or personality of their partner. And what I mean by this is that, one or both of the partners were caught in disbelief of the characteristics of their partner that they didn't know that their partner had. It's like, one or both of the partners started acting differently after they got married than how they used to act before they got married. You know, for example; maybe the partners used to be all lovey dovie before they got married, but as soon as they got married one or both of the partners starts acting mean and or uncaring towards each other. I mean it's crazy, but people can pretend to be all nice and caring before marriage, but then start showing their true mean and or uncaring selves after they marry. And this is why marriage is really a gamble, because a lot of people don't really reveal all about themselves until after marriage, you know, people tend to hide whatever shortcomings they may have until later after they are married is when their shortcoming starts to unveil itself, but by then they have already convinced someone that they are good for marriage, you know, that they are marriage material. And this is why it's very important for people to do their due diligence in examining the person they are thinking about marrying, because people can really surprise you with not only the amount of skeletons in their closets, but with their hidden character flaws.

And so yeah, a marriage can come crashing down not long after the Honeymoon if the couple doesn't start learning how to be married to each other. And learning how to be married to each other entails learning how to deal with each other and learning how to care and support each other. Learning how to deal, care, and support each other is what learning how to be married to each other is all about. These three factors are what will determine the success or failure of a marriage. Now, let's try to examine each one of these factors individually to see what each actually means and or entails more specifically.

The first factor is learning how to "deal" with each other: learning how to deal with each other is very crucial, because it sets the tone for how peaceful and or harmonious your household and your marriage will be. Learning how to deal with each other entails learning how to have patience and learning how to understand each other, so much so that the two of you don't get easily annoyed and or irritated with each other. Learning to deal with each other means learning how to handle any shortcomings and or bad habits that your partner may have. For example; if your partner is temperamental, you will learn how to calm your partner down without the conversation turning into a shouting match. Or, if your partner is very moody, you will know how to give them space or to cheer them up to reduce their moodiness. Or, if your partner is very stubborn, you will learn how to compromise with them and or agree to disagree with them so the situation doesn't turn into a big issue. Or, if your partner is kinda lazy, you will learn how to motivate them to get off their butts and do stuff, you know, you will know how to get them to help out around the house and such without complaining about how lazy they are all the time. Or, if your partner is a shopaholic, you will learn how to help them control their buying impulse. Or, if your partner is a heavy drinker, you will learn how to help them control their drinking so they don't end up being alcoholics, and if they do end up being alcoholics you will learn how to help them go get professional help (like; AA) so they can learn how to control their alcohol consumption. These are just a few examples of the kind of stuff that a couple may find themselves having to learn how to deal with about their partners. And learning how to deal with your spouse can take a lot of patience and sacrifice on your part, because some spouses can make it harder for their spouses to learn how to handle their shortcomings and or bad habits. But there's no other way around it, I mean, the couple has no choice but to learn how to deal with each other, because otherwise the marriage relationship can become very stressful and sooner than later one or both of the partner will decide they can't do it anymore, you know, they will decide that their partner is just too much to handle.

The second factor is learning how to "care" for each other: learning how to care for each other is very crucial, because it will give the couple an assurance and or a sense of knowing that they are truly loved by their partners. Because caring for each other entails looking out for each other, you know, taking the time to make sure that your spouse is ok all the time, and not just physically but also mentally and or emotionally. Caring for each other involves doing those things that will not only help reduce stress from your partner, but also doing those things that will increase joy in your partner, which in turn will help increase joy in the marriage. For example; if the wife has a rough day at her job and comes home feeling tired and exhausted, then the husband should go beyond the call of duty that evening with household responsibilities (getting dinner ready, washing dishes, getting the kids ready for bed, etc) so as to give the wife time to rest and unwind, so she can be rejuvenated for the next day of work. And the reverse is also the same, if the husband has a rough day at his job and comes home feeling tired and exhausted, then the wife should go beyond the call of duty that evening with the household responsibilities so as to give the husband time to rest and unwind, so he can be rejuvenated for the next day of work. So caring for each other is really about looking out for each other, you know, having each other's back. Caring for each other is paying attention to each other and seeing how each partner can help the other partner be less stressed and more joyous. Caring for each other is really just doing those extra little things that will make your spouse feel like they are being not only looked out for but will also make them feel loved and appreciated.

The third factor is learning how to "support" each other: learning how to support each other is very crucial, because it can help motivate the couple to aspire to be not just great husband and wife, but it can help them aspire to be great providers for the family both financially and emotionally. A lot of couples tend to not achieve much in life after they get married and it's because they tend not to get much support from their spouses. For example; if a wife wants to go back to school and get her masters degree but the husband doesn't really support the idea, most likely than not the wife won't go back to school to get her masters degree. Or, if the husband wants to start a business but the wife doesn't really support the idea, most likely than not the husband won't start a business. You see, spouses can really hinder their spouses growth and aspirations if they don't support each other. And what can happen is, one or both spouses can start resenting each other for not supporting each other's goals, dreams and or ambitions. It's very important for couples to try their best to support each other's dreams, goals and or aspirations, as long as those dreams, goals and aspirations won't interfere too much with the household's ability to continue to function properly, both financially and or emotionally. And what I mean by interfering with the household functioning properly is, the dreams, goals and aspirations won't put a huge financial or emotional burden on one or both of the partners, you know what I mean? It's not fair for a spouse to demand that they be supported on a dream, goal, or aspiration if it will put a huge burden on their spouse or on both of them. No, everything should be done sensibly, forcing things will do nothing but bring extra stress into the marriage. You should not have to force your spouse into supporting whatever dreams and or aspirations you may have, no, your spouse should want to support you because they love and care about you, therefore they want you to be the best you that you can be, and achieving success in whatever goals and aspirations a spouse may have usually increases joy and happiness for both partners, which in turn increases joy and happiness in the marriage.

Learning how to support each other in a marriage is very crucial, because it not only shows your spouse that you got their back, but it will also allow the two of you to increase your bond in the relationship. Because there's nothing like knowing that your partner has your back in whatever you are trying to achieve, because it makes you not only feel loved, but it also makes you feel more secure about your marriage relationship. And supporting each other doesn't have to be just on big things, no, even on little things, you know, like hobbies and such. For example; if the wife likes running and wants to train for a marathon, the husband should support her. Or, if the husband likes playing basketball and he wants to join a local recreational team, the wife should support him. Or, if the wife likes photography and wants to do it on the side, the husband should support her. Or, if the husband likes painting and would like to do painting on the side, the wife should support him. You see, there's a lot of things that people like to do but never do because they don't get the support from their spouses. Support can go a long way into making a partner feel loved, because there's nothing like knowing that someone you love also loves you so much that they want to try their best to support what you like to do, even little fun stuff. And a lot of times supporting each other actually helps in bringing the couple closer together, because they will be involved to some degree in whatever the other partner has interest in. Couples should really try to do as much stuff together, even if one of the partners is not really that interested in what the other partner is interested in, they should still make an attempt in participating in the hobbies of their partners. This is a great way of bonding, because it helps the couple spend much more time together and appreciate each other even more.

It's really about looking out for each other in a marriage, and trying your best to bring joy to your spouse rather than stress. As we all know, you can't really make another person happy in life, because happiness really starts within the person themselves, but you can try to bring some joy into your partner, from time to time. And this is why taking the time to hang out together doing the things that one or both of you like is very good, because it not only bring the two of you closer together, but it can help relieve some of whatever stress that may exist in one or both partners, as the two of you will be forced to leave the problems at home temporarily and go out and remind yourselves that you still love and care about each other. One thing that me and my wife like to do is to go to the movies every once in a while, since it's something that we both enjoy and it's something that we used to do before we got married, it reminds us of when we used to just hang out and have fun, even before we actually became a couple. We always reminisce about the movie we went to see together (GI Jane) which was the day that we realized that we really liked each other, you know, really liked each other for real for real, lol.

In a marriage, usually one partner will be more outgoing than the other. You know, one partner will be more of an adventurer than the other. So the partner who is less adventurous will tend to be more of a homebody than their partner, and will usually be the party pooper, you know, will be the one stopping the couple from doing a lot of fun things or activities, which can leave the outgoing partner feeling kinda bored and or miserable. So it behooves the less outgoing partner to try their best and support the more outgoing partner and join them on some fun and or adventures, because otherwise the more outgoing partner can start feeling bored and or miserable with the marriage, and may start becoming resentful in the relationship. Couples should really not limit each other, but they should support and uplift each other as much as possible.

And so yeah, couples really need to learn how to be married to each other, because if they don't, the marriage will suffer, and sooner than later divorce will follow. And you really don't want to get divorced do you? Of Course you don't, right? Because you didn't get married just for fun, right, you got married because you fell in love and wanted to spend the rest of your life with the person that you fell in love with, right!? Yes, that's why most people get married, it's because they want to spend the rest of their lives with the people they fall in love with. But a lot of people don't seem to want and or to have the ability to master the art of learning how to be married to their spouses, and this is why the divorce rate is so high, and it's because couples don't take the time to learn how to be married to each other. Marriage is not easy, it requires a lot of discipline, patience and a willingness to work to make it work, which becomes easier when both partners learn how to deal, care, and support each other, which is what learning how to be married to each other entails.

Okay, that's all I have for this chapter, I hope I did a good enough job of explaining what it takes to maintain a good functioning marriage, but if I didn't, I apologize, I will try to do a better job next time, but for now, let's move on to the next chapter that deals with what will happen if the couple doesn't learn how to be married to each other, which is, a divorce will happen!

6

DIVORCE

Divorce has to be one of the most saddest and or disappointing things for a couple to go through. And this is because it marks the ending of a couples marriage relationship, a relationship that they had vowed to be in till death do them part. But reality has hit, and one or both of the partners have realized that the marriage just isn't working, no matter how hard they have tried to make it work, they just can't seem to do so. So now, they seem to be left with no choice but to end their marriage, a decision they did not come by lightly. Deciding to end a marriage is not an easy decision, because there's a lot of pain and disappointment that can come with it. And the pain and disappointment can come not only to the divorcing couple, but it can also come to the couples friends and family. And what if the divorcing couple has children (which most usually do), how much more pain and disappointment would come to the children. And this is one of the reasons why most couples who have children delay ending a marriage and try to stick together for as long as they can, and it's because of the children, you know, it's because they know how much pain and disappointment the divorce will be on their children, so they try to hang in the marriage until the marriage becomes impossible to hang on to.

It is very hard to try to hang on to a marriage that is not working, especially if one of the partners doesn't seem like they have any interest in making it work. You know, it's like, one partner is still interested in trying to make it work by trying to be extra nice and or extra caring, but the other partner continues in their "I don't give a damn" attitude. Therefore after a while the partner that still wants to try and save the marriage ends up giving up and then sooner than later a divorce follows. Marriage is a lot of work, and it takes both partners actively wanting to make it work for it to have a chance of working. And sometimes both partners may want to try to make the marriage work but they just can't seem to be able to figure out what it is that they are doing wrong and or why they can't seem to get along and or how to go about fixing whatever the issues may be in their marriage. And this is where the help of a professional marriage counselor may be very helpful, because they can analyze the marriage with a professional eye and try to give the couple some good advice and or some good directions on how to proceed in their marriage to help make the marriage run more smoothly. But sometimes even marriage counseling can't help save a broken marriage, especially if one of the partners is not willing to take the advice of the counsellor, especially if that advice will require them to make some changes in their behavior and or actions. I don't know what it is, but a lot of people just don't like to make compromises and or make some changes about themselves that can be helpful in their relationship. And a marriage relationship requires a lot of compromises to be made by the partners so that they can be able to run their marriage more smoothly.

Marriage is hard work, it takes a lot of commitment, patience and a willingness to make it work, but it should get easier as time goes by and the couple learns how to be married to each other. Now, let's see if we can take a closer look at what can make a marriage breakdown and cause the couple to decide that they just can't do it anymore and decide to divorce. I will try to list some issues that can present themselves in a marriage that can cause problems for the couple if not dealt with correctly. The list will not be in any particular order, I will list them as they come to mind and I'll try my best to elaborate on them.

1. Religious Differences: it can be very hard for a couple to maintain a marriage for long if they belong to two different religions, especially if both of them are active or very active in their respective religions. For example; let's say one partner is Muslim and the other is Christian, and let's say both partners are active in their religion, that would mean the Muslim partner goes to the mosque to worship God on Friday and the Christian partner goes to church to worship God on Sunday, which means the couple will not be sharing the same worship and or sharing the same spirituality with each other, which can mean that the partners are not spiritually connected. Not being spiritually connected can be a huge deal in the marriage, because it will mean the partners are not spiritually united as one, you know, not spiritually united as one unit in the marriage. And not being spiritually united can be a challenge, because faith is very important to a religious person, and so even though the couple may respect each other's religion when they are just dating, when it comes to marriage the difference can be a hindrance in the growth of their marriage, because they won't be totally united in mind, body and spirit, as a marriage should be.

Also, raising children can turn out to be kind of an extra challenge for a married couple with two different religions, because each partner will want the children to learn and or practice their religion. And so, deciding how to maneuver this situation so that both partners can feel satisfied with the children learning and practicing each partner's religion can be a huge challenge, which can bring about a lot of confusion in the household. This is why it's very important for partners who belong to different religions to discuss how they are going to raise their children spiritually before they get married, so as to try and reduce the extra confusion in raising their children, otherwise they can easily find themselves in a spiritual marriage mess.

But usually most couples who belong to different religions will get one of the partners to convert to the other partner's religion before they get married, that way both of them will belong to the same religion, that way they can be spiritually connected in their marriage. And usually, couples who don't convert to one partner's religion but each keeps their own religion, they usually tend to be not active in their respective religions, you know, the Muslim partner doesn't go to the mosque or pray five times a day, and the Christian partner doesn't go to church or have crosses all over the house. And sometimes one partner may be active but the other partner not so active in their respective religions, and the non active partner will tend to support the active partner to some degree without converting. But the whole thing can be very tricky and very challenging to the marriage, especially if both partners are active in their respective religions.

This religious difference being a hindrance to a marriage can also be true of two Christians who belong to different denominations, you know, like if one is Catholic and one is Seventh Day Adventist. Because that would mean one partner will be worshipping God on Sunday (Catholic) and one partner will be worshipping God on Saturday (Seventh Day Adventist). And then when they have children, which denomination will they raise their children in? Or will they try to get their children to belong and practice both denominations? See how tricky partners having religious differences can be in a marriage. This is why most people who fall in love with someone with a different religion from them, they will either convert to their partner's religion or try to get their partner to convert to theirs, because they know if they are not spiritually connected their marriage may have a hard time working out.

2. No Pre-marital Counseling: not having pre-marital counseling is like jumping into a marriage with no clue of what a marriage is all about and or how to navigate through it. Pre-marital Counseling is very important, because it forces the couple to actually talk about the marriage in a serious way and start planning how they are going to operate in it, you know, how they are going to handle the responsibilities that come with being married. Like for example; how are they going to pay the bills, will they have a joint account or maintain separate accounts, what about saving money, what about children, how many children and will one of them be a stay at home mom or dad, and what about buying a house, and etc and etc. There's just so much stuff that comes up in a marriage that if the couple is not prepared they can really find themselves shell shocked and getting frustrated with the marriage very early into their marriage. Pre-marital Counseling can really help to eliminate a lot of the surprises that can pop up in a marriage that the couple didn't even think about. Without pre-marital counseling, that will mean that the couple will pretty much have to figure out how they are going to deal with things as they go, which can be a challenge if they haven't yet learned how each other likes to operate and or do things. And if their communication is not good, they can easily start finding themselves being frustrated with each other, which in the long run can hinder their marriage from growing positively, which can cause their marriage to have a hard time working out.

3. Financial Issues: arguing about money is one of the biggest reasons I think why most marriages don't work, because money problems tend to always be around, you know, money problems just seem to never end. I wonder if rich people have money issues, you know, I wonder if rich people have arguments over money as us regular broke folks do, you know what I mean, lol. They probably do, but they probably get in arguments over money when one of the partners has spent tens of thousands of dollars on Amazon in a month, unlike us regular broke folks who will argue intensely with our spouse over one of us spending a hundred dollars on Amazon in a month, lol. But hey, that one hundred dollars can feel like tens of thousands of dollars when you broke and you have a hundred dollar bill payment that is already past due, right? I totally understand, every couple's money spending habit and or threshold has to match their income level and household budget needs. So you can't just spend a hundred dollars on Amazon in a month for recreational purchases if your household budget needs that hundred dollars to pay bills. And this is how a lot of couples tend to find themselves arguing over money, and it's because one of the partners tends to not be good and or disciplined on how to not carelessly spend money, especially if their household is operating on a tight budget.

In a marriage, usually there will be one partner who is more of a saver and extra careful with how they spend money and there will be a partner who is not much of a saver and is kind of carefree about spending money. And what tends to happen is, the partner that is extra careful about how they spend money will tend to get irritated with how carefree the other partner is about spending money. This is why it's important for couples to come up with a plan and or formula of how they are going to manage their household income, otherwise fighting over money will never end. The best formula I think in managing household income is for the couple to have a joint account for paying bills and for savings, and then have separate individual accounts for discretionary income for each partner. The discretionary income is any money that is left over after the money for paying bills and for saving is allocated and or deposited into the joint accounts. And so in this method, the couple will need to know what their average monthly total household expenses are. They will have to calculate everything, you know, like: rent/mortgage, car payment, car insurance, health insurance, groceries, cell phones, electric/gas bill, water bill, etc and etc, all household expenses. And then once they know their average monthly household expenses, they will allocate enough money from their combined income (if both of them work) into their joint account to cover their expenses. And then they will allocate a percentage of their combined income to go into their joint savings account. And then whatever money is left is their discretionary income which they can split half and half and each partner can do whatever they want with their share of the discretionary income. You know, if the husband wants to go buy a guitar even though he doesn't know how to play it, oh well, the wife shouldn't fuss about it, it's his discretionary money, he can buy whatever he wants with it, even if the wife thinks the guitar is wasteful spending. And likewise, if the wife wants to go buy another handbag even though she already has a whole lot of handbags in the closet, oh well, the husband shouldn't fuss about it, it's her discretionary money, she can buy whatever she wants with it, even if the husband thinks the handbag is wasteful spending.

You see, there's ways to try and reduce money arguments in a marriage. It's all about making a plan and or coming up with a method of managing household income that will allow for each partner to still feel like they can spend some extra money that they may have without the other partner fussing about it. So really it's all about discipline, to be able to stick to the plan. But unfortunately there's a lot of couples who are not disciplined enough to stick to the plan, you know, couples where one partner has a habit of dipping into the joint account that's for paying bills or the joint account that is for savings, and they will use the money to make a discretionary purchase, you know, they will make a purchase that is not an absolutely necessary, and they will most often do it without first talking to their spouses about it. And this is how most fights about money come about, and it's when one of the partners has spend money that was allocated for something else, and they spend it without consulting with their spouse first to try and see if it was ok for them to take the money out and perhaps replace it as soon as possible from their next paycheck. But this is how money fights come about, one partner spends money they shouldn't be spending, and when their spouse finds out about it, it ends up becoming a big fight. It's all about discipline and communication, especially if the couple is going through a tough financial period, this is when both partners have to be extra disciplined with how they spend money, because chances are there won't be any discretionary money available during tough times, so extra care has to be taken on how household income is spent, otherwise fights over money will become an endless situation.

So it's all about planning and sticking to the plan when it comes to managing household income. And it doesn't matter whether the couple is rich or poor when it comes to managing household income, because rich people fight over money too. I'm pretty sure you have heard of celebrities who have divorced because one partner was either overspending or one partner kept making bad investments, or one partner had a secret account that they didn't tell the other partner about. Most rich people don't spend money all willy neely, no, they tend to have budgets and they tend to require their spouses to stay within budget. Money is money at the end of the day and most people don't want to waste it on unnecessary spending, no matter if they are rich or poor. So the trick in trying to reduce money fights is to have a plan and to be disciplined enough for each partner to stick to the plan, because fighting over money can get very tiring after a while, which can lead to a breakdown in the relationship, and in which can cause one or both partners to give up on the marriage.

4. Cheating/Infidelity: I think infidelity may be the biggest reason for why most marriages end in divorce. And the reason I say this is because, for one; it seems like most guys have a hard time taming their hunting nature after they get married and end up cheating on their wives sooner than later. And for two; it seems like wives nowadays have adopted a zero tolerance policy on cheating husbands, you know, wives are not accepting being cheated on by their husbands anymore, you know, unlike the wives of previous generations did, you know what I mean? And what I mean is (just to be clearer), wives in past generations tolerated their husbands being unfaithful to them much more than wives in these current generations. And the reason why wives in past generations were more tolerant of their cheating husbands is because back in those days most women were stay at home moms, and so they depended very heavily on the financial support of their husbands. And so wives were kinda stuck in their marriages even if the husbands were not being faithful to their wives their wives couldn't just get out and move out and divorce their husbands. Because back in those days it was very hard for women to establish themselves financially, because there were not a lot of careers and or employment opportunities for women back in past generations. And so husbands could be unfaithful to their wives and their wives just had to accept it, you know, because they didn't have much option financially to be able to leave and divorce their husbands. But nowadays, forget about it, women are not playing games with men anymore, wives are not having it, no, nowadays wives have zero tolerance for cheating husbands. I mean, just one cheat and the husband can find himself being divorced by his wife, just one cheat, that's it, and the marriage can be over. Whew, women are not playing around nowadays, no, not at all, they would rather be by themselves then have an unfaithful husband.

And the reason why women can have a zero tolerance on unfaithful husbands is because nowadays women are not so dependent on men financially as women were back in generations past. Nowadays most women enter into a marriage with financial means, sometimes with more means than their husbands. And this is why nowadays most wives are not stuck in their marriages based on depending on their husbands financially, because nowadays wives not only usually enter their marriages with their own financial means, but they have more opportunity to attain their own financial means if they divorce their husbands. And so this is one of the main reasons why a lot of marriages end in divorce nowadays, and it's because wives are not tolerating their husbands' infidelity any more, like they did back in the days. But unfortunately, husbands are still finding themselves having affairs and cheating on their wives, for whatever reasons. Now, of course wives do have affairs and cheat on their husbands too, but the ratio is way more husbands cheat on their wives than wives cheating on their husbands, am I right or wrong? But, cheating is cheating, no matter who does it, the husband or the wife, it's still wrong and it's the fastest road to a divorce than anything else.

Now, let's examine and discuss what may be the reasons that a husband and or a wife may find themselves having an affair and or cheating on their spouses. There are really only two reasons why a spouse may cheat; the first reason is what I like to call **Seek for lust cheating.** In seek for lust cheating, the cheating partner cheats on their spouse because of lust. You know, they allow themselves to lust after other people that they find to be sexually desirable and before long they decide to pursue and engage in some extra marital affairs with the people that they desire sexually. It's a lust thing and not being able to tame and or control one's sexual desire for another person that is not their spouse. Learning how to tame and or control their lust is one of the hardest things that men have to learn how to do when they are in a relationship. And this is because men are hunters by nature and hunting for sex comes very natural to men, you know, when a man sees a sexually desirable woman his instinct is to pursue her and see if she will be willing to go engage in some sexual activity with him, you know what I mean? And so, when a man gets in a relationship he has to work extra hard to learn how to tame and or control his sex hunting ways, which can be very hard, especially if he hasn't learned how to not put himself in situations where he can be easily tempted. It takes a lot of discipline for a man to learn how to admire and or appreciate a sexy woman without wanting to pursue her sexually, it takes a continuous conscious effort of him reminding himself that it is not worth it to pursue another woman and cheat on his wife. But it doesn't take much effort for a man to end up finding himself succumbing to his lust and end up cheating on his spouse, and it's because there's so much temptation out there, you know, there are just so many women who have no problem sleeping with married men. I mean, I don't know what it is, but it seems like women have a thing for married men, it's like men become more attractive (to other women) when they are married.

I remember when I was newly married (first or second year), I was at the DMV (department of motor vehicle) in Largo Maryland, getting tags for my car, I had already got the tags and I was outside putting the tags on my car, when this sexy young lady came by my car and asked me if I could help her put her tags on her car when I'm done with mine. I said, ok, sure. Then when I was done, I walked over to her car and started putting her tags on her car. We did some chatting as I was putting her tags on. I don't remember much of our conversation, but I remember her telling me that she is in the process of moving out from her and her boyfriend's place because the relationship was terrible. And she said that she was planning on moving out before her boyfriend got back home in a few days (her boyfriend was a long distance truck driver). I told her sorry to hear that and maybe moving out may be a good idea if the relationship is terrible. Then when I was finished putting her tags on and getting ready to say bye to her, she asked me if I would like to come over to her place and help her move. I told her sorry I won't be able to. Then she took a piece of paper and wrote her number on it (this was before cell phones were a thing) and handed it to me and told me that if I change my mind to give her a call. I looked at her for a few seconds and just smiled. She had a look on her face that let me know that she wasn't really just asking me to go help her move, no, she was actually inviting me to her place for some extra curricular activity of the sexual kind, you know what I mean? She had really caught me off guard, I didn't know what to do or say, as I stood there with her number in my hand. I don't remember the rest of the conversation, but I remember walking back to my car with her number in my hand thinking to myself, wow, I can't believe I've just been offered some sexual healing just like that. And I couldn't believe that she didn't even care that I was married (I had my wedding ring on and it was very visible).

So I stood there by my car for a little bit thinking, this is trouble, I should not be even slightly entertaining the thought of maybe I should call her and see what happens. For a few seconds there I found myself being tempted to pursue the invitation for sexual healing, because I am not even gonna lie, the young lady was very sexy, and my natural instinct as a man to hunt for sexual healing was awoken by her. But I quickly came to my senses and realized that her temptation was nothing but trouble. You know, I had no business even entertaining the thought of calling her and seeing what would happen. Because what would happen is, I would sneak around and call her and she would put that sexy voice that women put on over the phone to get a guy all excited (you know, horny) and to want to get with them even more. And I had a feeling that I probably would not be able to resist her temptation if I did call her, and sooner than later I would have ended up at her place and ended up engaging in some extracurricular activity (sex) that I have no business engaging with her on. But thankfully I quickly came to my senses and decided to just throw her number away before I got myself into trouble.

You see how easy it is for a married person to find themselves facing some extramarital temptations, it can happen just like that. A guy can be minding his own business and a sexy woman can walk by and glance at the guy and the guy can find himself starting to lust after the woman. Now imagine if the sexy woman actually walked up to the guy and give him her phone number and gave him the look that said that she is ready willing and able to give him some loving (sex), can you imagine how hard that may be for the guy to resist. But, as married people we just have to learn how to resist extra marital temptations, no matter how hard the temptation may be to resist. Two of the best ways to help in resisting temptation from someone whom you know has the hots for you and you think they are sexy, is to one; play avoidance, and two; don't take or give them your number. You know, try your best not to run into them, that way they won't have the opportunity to tempt you, or to tempt you as much. Because sometimes it's hard to totally avoid people, especially if they are co-workers. And so the best you can do is to try your best not to run into them, so you won't give them a chance to engage you in a conversation that can turn out to be very tempting, to where you start to want to get to know them some more, you know what I mean? And for two, you definitely should not give or take their phone number, because if you do, the temptation to call them or if they call you the temptation for you to answer their call may be too great for you to resist. So play avoidance and make sure you don't take or give your number to someone whom you know has the hots for you, and whom you may find to be sexually desirable, because if you do, you may quickly find yourself in some extra marital affair that will do nothing but cause trouble in your marriage.

So anyway, **seek for lust cheating** is one of the reasons why people cheat on their spouses, and it's because they have not learned how to tame their sexual desires for other people they find sexually desirable and end up pursuing those people and end up cheating on their spouses.

The other reason why a husband or a wife may find themselves having an affair and cheating on their spouse is what I like to call: **Need for lust cheating.** In this type of cheating, the cheating spouse usually has some kind of need that is not being met at home with their spouse that they find themselves looking for it in another person. In need for lust cheating, it's not really lust that actually drives the spouse to cheat, no, it's their desire to fill an emptiness that has developed in their marriage that forces them to go seek to fill that emptiness with someone else. And a lot of times the cheating spouse doesn't actually seek out to cheat in this type of cheating, the cheating usually happens while they are trying to fill an emptiness. It's like, for example; if a spouse does not feel loved and or appreciated at home by their partner, they can find themselves cheating on their partner with someone whom they don't even find to be that sexy, but because that person makes them feel loved and appreciated, somehow the cheating spouse allows themselves to get romantically involved with the person that is making them feel loved and appreciated. And this is one of the biggest reasons why most married people cheat on their spouses and have affairs, and it's because they are trying to fill an emptiness that has developed in their marriage. These emptiness are usually caused by the partners not paying attention to each other and end up neglecting each other. You know, the partners don't take the time to make sure that they reassure their love and appreciation for each other. Now, of course, reassuring each other's love and appreciation for each other can be hard to do when there's a lot of friction and or turmoil in the marriage. Friction and or turmoil in a marriage is what can cause couples not to pay attention to each other and start neglecting each other, which if not corrected and or if not remedied in a timely manner, it can make one or both of the partners start to feel lonely and or unloved in the marriage and then result in starting to look for that love and attention elsewhere.

You see, the sex part in **need for lust cheating** usually is the after result of neglect and or a partner not feeling loved in their marriage, unlike in the seek for lust cheating, where the partner is looking to cheat whenever an opportunity presents itself, no matter if their partner at home gives them attention and or shows them love, the seek for lust cheater is motivated to cheat based on their desire to lust other people. But the need for lust cheater is motivated to cheat based on being neglected and or not feeling loved in their marriage. Now, of course cheating is bad either way, you know, cheating is cheating and there's no excuse and or reason that can make it okay to do it. But unfortunately it happens a lot, and this is because for one; there's just so many temptations out there, and for two; there's a lot of marriages that have friction in them that results in making one or both partners feel neglected and or unloved by their spouses. And so, these two reasons are the main reasons why most spouses may find themselves cheating on their partners, and it's because of either their inability to tame their lust for others, and or it's because they feel neglected and or unloved by their partners.

And so, infidelity is one of the biggest reasons why most marriages end in divorce. And it's because infidelity brings with it a lot of pain and disappointment into the marriage. And this is because when a partner cheats, they will have broken the vowel that they had given to their partner of forsaking all others and being with only them, in mind, body, and spirit. But when a partner cheats, that means they have given some and or all of themselves to another, which means they have betrayed their partner in whom they vowed and or promised to only be with them (forsaking all others). And the betrayal brings with it a lot of pain and disappointment, because now trust will have been broken, you know, the cheating partner will cause their spouse to have a hard time trusting them again. And trust is everything in a marriage, without trust, it will be very hard for the marriage to work out, because a marriage without trust amongst the partners can do nothing but bring more stress and misery into the marriage, because the partners will not be secure in their relationship, as they won't feel like they can truly trust each other anymore.

Infidelity is the worst thing that a partner can do in a marriage, because it involves intimacy, you know, it involves giving another person a very sacred activity (sex) that is supposed to be reserved only for their spouse. And this is why it is usually very hard for a couple to reconcile and or forgive the person who committed the infidelity, and it's because the thought of a spouse being with another person is just very heartbreaking for the cheated on spouse. Because sex is actually a very sacred act, it is something that connects two individuals together bodily. And so the thought of a spouse connecting with someone else bodily is a very hard thing for a partner to take in. And this is why a lot of marriages where an infidelity occurs tend to have a hard time working out, even if the cheated spouse forgives the cheating spouse, and it's because the infidelity has kind of tainted the purity of the couple's bond, not just physically, but also mentally and emotionally. You see, sex in a marriage is a very sacred thing, it's not just for pleasure, no, it's also an emotional connector between the couple, it's what brings the couple even more closer to each other both physically and emotionally. And so when an infidelity occurs in the marriage, the couple's physical and emotional connection will suffer, because their physical and emotional connector (sex) will have been tainted, because it will have been shared with someone else. And this has nothing to do with whether the couple were virgins or not when they got married, no, because the purity of a marriage begins when the couple says I Do to each other, that's when the purity of their marriage begins. And so if one partner ends up cheating on the other partner after they are married, the cheating partner will have tainted the purity of their marriage, because they will have shared themselves with someone else a part of themselves that they were only supposed to share with their spouse.

Infidelity is not an easy thing for a marriage to overcome, because it brings a lot of pain and disappointment to the cheated spouse. And this pain and disappointment doesn't go away very easily, and perhaps it doesn't really ever go away. Because every time the cheated spouse thinks about it, I'm pretty sure the pain and disappointment comes right back into their heart and mind. And I mean, it could have been five or ten years later, but to the cheated spouse, the cheating can seem like it just happened not that long ago, and this is because emotional pain tends to last a lot longer than any other kinds of pain, and the feelings of it can feel like it just happened not that long ago.

And so, Infidelity is very detrimental to a marriage, it's something that should be avoided, no matter how hard the avoidance may seem to be to do, the partners should really try their best to avoid it, because otherwise, a divorce won't be far away, because very few marriages can survive an infidelity.

5. In-laws: most couples who get married don't realize that not only are they marrying their partners, but they don't realize that they are also marrying their partner's family as well, so to speak, you know what I mean? Because it's like, your partner has a family, and her family still wants to be a part of your partner's life even after she is married to you. And the reverse is also true, you have a family, and your family still wants to be in your life even after you get married. And so, since your partner will still be involved with their family, that means you too will have to be involved with your partners family, to some extent. And the reverse is also true, since you will still be involved with your family, then that means your partner will have to be involved with your family also, to some extent. Now, the extent of how much a spouse has to be involved with their in-laws depends on how much their spouse is involved with their family. For example; if one of the partners tends to visit their family a lot or if their partner's family members tend to come to visit their partner a lot, then that will mean the spouse will have to visit their partner's family a lot too, and or the spouse will have to deal with their partner's family coming over to the couple's home a lot.

Now, of course there's nothing wrong with going to visit in-laws or in-laws coming to visit the couple, but the couple has to be careful in how much visits they engage in or allow at their homes from their in-laws, especially if their in-laws are crazy and or if their in-laws don't seem to understand the concept of boundaries. There's nothing worse than having in-laws that are either crazy nuts or in-laws that want to be all up in a couple's marriage. You know, in-laws that want to know everything that is going on in a couple's marriage, you know, nosy and or intrusive in-laws. These kinds of in-laws should be avoided as much as possible, because they can very easily start to bring friction between the couple, especially if some of the in-laws decide they don't like the partner that their loved one is married to, you know what I mean?

Learning how to deal and or manage in-laws can be a very tricky situation, because in one hand these are your spouse's parents and relatives, and you want them to be happy about the union between you and their loved one, but at the same time, you don't want them to be all up in your marriage calling shots, you know, trying to run your marriage. Because most often, if your in-laws are all up in your marriage, the in-laws will want to control and or influence how things are run in your household, even on how to raise your children. You know, it's like, a mother-in-law may want the daughter-in-law to take care of the household just like how the mother-in-law took take of her own household, but then, if the daughter-in-law doesn't take care of the household like how her mother-in-law wants her to, a big friction can develop between the mother-in-law and the daughter-in-law and this friction can cause the spouses to also have friction between them because of the mother-in-law. There's mothers in-laws out there who just don't know how to stay out of their loved one's marriages, you know, they just want to know everything and influence how things are run in their loved one's marriages. Now, it's okay if parents want to offer advice to their loved one's to help support the marriage, but parents and or other in-laws should not be making final decisions on how their loved one's marriage and or household is run, no, the final decision on how a household is run should be left to the couple. Because just imagine if in-laws from both sides of the couple are all up in their loved one's marriage and each side wants the couple's marriage and household to be run how each in-law thinks it should be run, can you imagine the amount of confusion and or friction that can come out of that.

And so, couples really need to be careful with how much involvement and or say they allow their in-laws to have in their marriage, the lesser the better. In-laws actually should just be close outside supporters of the couple, not outside directors of the couples. And couples need to make sure that they themselves don't invite their parents and or relatives to be all up in their marriage by sharing everything that goes on in their marriage with their parents and or relatives. And what I mean is, couples should not run to their parents and or relatives and tell them about all the problems that they may be going through in their marriage, couples should really try to solve whatever problems and or issues that may be present in their marriage by themselves or by getting counsel from a non-relative or from a professional marriage counselor. Now, I'm not saying that you shouldn't tell your parents and or relatives anything about how the marriage is going, no, I'm saying don't tell them everything, you know, you have to be very selective on how much the two of you are willing to share with your families and with your in-laws. Now, if you are in a toxic marriage, then of course you want your family to know about it, because you are going to need your family to give you the strength to get out of that kind of a marriage. And what is a toxic marriage, it's a marriage where one or both partners are treating each other like trash, you know, a marriage where the partners seem to have lost respect and or love for each other and all they seem to do is argue and fight all the time, and or a marriage where there is physical and or emotional abuse. No one needs to stay in a toxic marriage, and in this type of situation, parents and relatives definitely need to know how bad the marriage is, so that they can help their loved ones to find the strength to get out of the marriage.

Dealing with in-laws can be a challenge, but if the couple set the tone and or set the boundaries early, and if the couple has each other's back if situations with in-laws arises, the couple should not have too much trouble dealing with their in-laws, because the in-laws will know that the couple is unified and doesn't allow intrusiveness in their marriage. But this tone and boundaries has to be set very early in the marriage, because if not, it won't take long for the in-laws to try and assert themselves in their loved one's marriage and become intrusive. Dealing with in-laws can be easy or hard, it all depends on what kind of in-laws a couple inherits, because some families are cool and peaceful people, but there's families that are kinda crazy and or nuts. But, you fell in love with their loved one, and now you have no choice but to deal with their extended family, which can be a pleasant or an ugly experience, but either way the couple should be unified on how they deal with their in-laws, because if they are not, they can easily find themselves fighting with each other over their in-laws all the time, which can bring a lot of friction into the marriage, even to the point of ruining their marriage.

And so yeah, dealing with in-laws can be a challenge, but if the couple is unified, in-laws will have no choice but to respect their loved one's marriage and learn how to become outside supporters of their loved one's marriage, instead of trying to be outside directors of their loved one's marriage.

6. The Thrill is Gone: when a couple gets married, there tends to be a lot of passion and excitement in their relationship in the early years, but that passion and excitement tends to reduce as the years go by. And sometimes that passion and excitement can reduce so much that the couple can start living like roommates, you know, the partners hardly speak, and they walk around the house doing their own things, and passion and romance hardly exists in the marriage anymore. A marriage can really lose its luster if the couple is not careful and or not paying attention. And what I mean by not paying attention is, the couple is not paying attention to how the marriage is evolving through the years, you know, the couple is not paying attention to see if the two of them are still growing together as the years go by or do they seem to be growing apart. Couples growing apart is a real thing, and it usually creeps up on couples without them really noticing, and by the time they realize it, it can be too late to reignite the marriage, as the marital flame will have died out.

It is very important for couples to try and maintain some kind of level of passion and excitement in their marriage. Did you notice how I said "some kind of level" of passion and excitement? And the reason I said "some kind of level" is because, as time goes by, the couple will be so used to seeing each other, and so used to being around each other, and so used to being intimate with each other, that over time they won't be as passionate over each other as they were when they first got married. It's a natural thing that happens. You know, it's like, for example; people do get overly excited about things when they first get them, but then after they have played with and or being around those things for a long while, their passion and or excitement over those things will go down. It doesn't mean that they no longer want to play with those things and or be around those things, no, it just means they are not as excited over those things as they once were, you know, not as excited as when they first got them. And so the same is as with a marriage, when a couple first gets married, their excitement and passion levels are so high. This is why in that first year of marriage most couples look like they can't keep their hands off each other, you know what I mean? And this is because they are so excited to finally be together and to live together, and to see each other everyday, and to make love to each other as much as they want, morning, noon, or night, anytime when the mood hits, and it will hit a lot, why, because they are so full of passion and excitement for each other.

Now, of course this high level of passion and excitement in a marriage is very hard to maintain throughout the marriage, because as time goes on, a couple will be used to seeing each other everyday, used to living together, used to making love to each other, that their passion and excitement for each other will naturally start to go down. Also, the busyness of life (jobs, children, etc) will reduce the time and energy for the couple to want to do much (adventure wise), especially when they start to have children. Raising children is a lot of work, it requires a lot of time and energy, so much so that a couple can find themselves to being too tired and exhausted to do much else, you know, even too tired and exhausted to have sex. And this is one of the ways in which a couple can find themselves in a sex-less marriage, and it's because one or both partners can find themselves feeling too tired all the time that the desire to have sex can diminish a lot. And this is why it's important for both partners to be fully involved in the raising of the children. You know, both partners should be hands on helping each other with the children everyday, that way neither partner will feel overwhelmed with taking care of the children.

Jobs and raising children can really leave a couple feeling too tired to have sex, that's why couples have to learn how to make time for them to spend some quality time together. And that quality time doesn't have to be a whole day affair, even an hour of quality time can work magic for a couple. Imagine making love for an hour with your spouse, how wonderful would that be, and how much of that loving feeling would that bring into the marriage. Did you notice how I said "love making for an hour" instead of "sex for an hour"? I did that on purpose. And the reason why I did that is because, there's a difference between making love for an hour and just having sex for an hour. And the difference is, love making involves a couple taking their time with each other, you know, they take things slow with the sexual healing, you know, love making involves slow touchy touchy and slow kissy kissy while they are having sex. Love making is sex that is not rushed, it's sex that usually starts with some foreplay, it's sex that finds the couple looking into each other's eyes while enjoying some gentle sexual healing. How much marital flames do you think a couple would gain for their marriage if they engaged in this kind of sexual healing (love making) from time to time. They would gain a lot of flames for their marriage, right!?

It is very important for couples to consciously make an effort to keep their marital flame going by doing those activities that will bring them closer together, you know, things that will make them express and share that loving feeling towards each other. It's all about spending some quality time with each other as much as possible, even if the quality time is not a whole day affair, or even if the quality time does not involve sex, it's all good as long the two of you are doing it together. Some examples of spending quality time together doing simple activities can be; watching a Netflix movie together while hugging up on the couch, or, taking a walk together while engaging on some nice conversation, or, going to the gym and working out together, or, gardening together, or washing the car together, or, cooking dinner together, or, doing laundry together, and etc. You know, it's about being close together and enjoying each other's company. Because truth be told, life can be so busy and hectic sometimes that couples can find themselves so wrapped up with their jobs, and with their kids, and with other stuff, that they can end up ignoring each other without intending to, and then after a while they can lose that close connection that they had when they first got married. So couples really need to make a conscious effort to make time to spend some quality time with each other, no matter how hectic their lives may be, because otherwise they can wake up one day and realize that the flame in their marriage is gone, as they will start to see and live with each other more like roommates than lovers. And once a couple starts to see and live with each other more like roommates than lovers, their marriage will be in danger, because that will mean there will be no intimacy in the marriage, and if there's no intimacy in the marriage, the marriage will be in danger of collapsing sooner or later. And this is because intimacy is what usually helps to keep a marriage strong, as the couple will be connected, because intimacy is a great connector of people. And intimacy can be as simple as holding hands and or hugging up on each other.

And so yeah, it's very important for couples to try and maintain some kinda level of passion and excitement in their marriage, and this has to be a conscious effort by both partners, you know, one partner shouldn't just wait for the other partner to initiate the passion and or excitement in their marriage, no, both partners should make efforts in initiating passion and excitement into their marriage. Because if one partner just waits for the other partner to initiate passion and excitement in their marriage all the time, what do you think will happen if the partner that usually does the initiating starts to find themselves being too tired and or too busy to do the passion and excitement initiating? There probably won't be much passion and excitement going on in that marriage anymore, right? And so this is why it's important for both partners to make the effort to do the passion and excitement initiating in their marriage, you know, so they can be balanced in maintaining the passion and excitement in their marriage, instead of just depending on one partner to be the initiator of passion and excitement in their marriage.

Marriage is not an easy institution, the success of it doesn't just happen by itself, no, the partners have to actually work at it, especially when it comes to maintaining passion and excitement in the marriage, because it's just so easy for one or both of the partners to start ignoring each other consciously and or subconsciously, for whatever reason. And ignoring each other usually tends to lead to having a marriage with no passion and or excitement in it, and that usually tends to lead to the partners to start feeling unhappy in their marriage. Passion and excitement for each other is what usually brings two people together to fall in love and get married to each other, but the lack of passion and or excitement in a marriage is what usually breaks a couple apart, and causes them to end up divorcing sooner than later. Because who wants to be in a boring and passionless marriage, not me, do you? I don't think you do either!

So it's very important for a couple to continue to do those little things that will keep their marital flame going, because it can be so easy to lose that flame, especially if the partners are not as attractive as they used to be when they first got married, lol, you know what I mean? Hey hey hey, I'm just trying to keep it real here, we all lose some of our attractiveness as we age, you know, our bodies start sagging and all that kinda stuff, lol. I mean, am I right or wrong? Don't our bodies tend to change some as we get older? Yes it does, no matter how much exercise we do, our bodies won't stay the same as when we were younger, it's just part of the natural state of aging. It's like for example; when men age their bodies tend to get wider and their muscles tend to get softer, and many men tend to grow beer bellies. And when women age their bodies tend to get…....you know what, I really don't know what tends to happen to women's bodies as they age, I think women stay sexy and gorgeous always to old age, lol. You see there, did you catch what I just did? I just caught myself and escaped getting myself into trouble by not mentioning what happens to women's bodies as they age, did you catch that, smart move on my part, because I know women don't like men talking about their bodies, and I would have caught some heat from some of the women that would read this book, wisdom prevailed on my part, woo hoo, pat on the back, lol.

Anyway, I think you understand what I'm trying to say, which is, as we get older, our bodies change somewhat, some more than others. And so, the initial physical attraction that we had for our spouses when we first met them can change over time to us no longer having the same attraction or the same level of attraction to no attraction anymore, if we don't continue to ignite passion into our marriages. Over time, our spouses will change somewhat physically, but if we continue to be intimate with them, we will get used to being with them and to make love to them even if their physical appearance is not the same as when we first got married to them. You know, for example; a wife will get used to making love to her husband even if he is now kinda wide and has a beer belly. And a husband will get used to making love to his wife even if she is now kinda wide and has…….., I will let you fill in the blank, not trying to get in trouble, no no no, lol. I think you get the point, it's important for a couple to continue to be intimate with each other as much as possible in their marriage, so they won't lose that loving feeling towards each other, you know, so they won't lose the sexual attraction towards each other, because if they do, it will be very hard for the marriage to survive, because the thrill for each other will be gone, and when the thrill is gone, divorce usually tends to follow sooner than later!

Divorce is the sad ugly result of what happens when a couple does not learn how to be married to each other. They say fifty percent of all marriages end in divorce, and I think that number may be a little low, I think it's more like sixty or seventy percent of all marriages end in divorce. And the reason why I say sixty or seventy percent, it's because when I look around at people I know who are of marriage age, there are a lot of people who have been divorced before. And most people nowadays tend to be products of divorced parents, you know, their parents divorced when they were still kids. I mean it's crazy, but it seems like a lot of couples don't seem to be able to make their marriage work out. I mean, just think about your own surroundings and or the people in your own family. How many marriages are still going strong past 20 years, past 30 years, probably not many, right? And how many people and or family members who have been divorced before, that you know of? You probably know a lot of people who have been divorced before? It's crazy, but marriage is a lot of work, it requires a lot of patience, understanding, and commitment to each other. I myself had to learn patience (I used to be very impatient), I had to learn how to understand my wife better (I used to not be a very good listener), I had to learn how to totally commit to my wife (I thank God for giving me wisdom in this regard). Marriage is not easy, but it doesn't have to be that hard either, it's all about the couple understanding each other and looking out for each other. That's it, when a couple truly understands each other (how each thinks and or operates), and they go out of their way to look out for each other, it will make the marriage a lot easier to manage and or to be in. But learning how to truly understand each other can take time, because the couple has to truly learn and accept each other's personalities and learn how to function as one unit, which can take time if one or both partners haven't learned how to be married to each other yet.

Divorce is a sad state of affairs for a couple, it brings with it a lot of pain and disappointment, not just for the couple, but for everyone who knows and loves the couple. And it's almost like, when a couple divorces, not only are they divorcing their spouses, it's almost like they're divorcing their spouses family and friends as well. And this is why a lot of couples usually stay together longer than they need to in their not working out marriages, and it's because they feel bad to have to disappoint a whole lot of people whom they have come to love and have become part of their family. And if the couple has children, a divorce becomes even more sad to do, because the children will definitely feel tremendously hurt that their parents couldn't stay married to each other. And this is why a lot of parents will tend to stay longer even in a toxic marriage, and it's because they don't want to take their children through the pain of separation through divorce, because divorces can turn ugly, and children can be dragged through it and be left with great emotional scars. But, when a marriage is over, it's over. Because there's nothing anybody can do to save a marriage that is totally not working, especially if the marriage is toxic.

So, good people, take care of each other out there, if you are married, take care of your spouse, marriage is all about spouses looking out for each other, that's the best way to show each other that you care about each other, which will bring more joy into the marriage. We need to see more joyous marriages, not more divorces, so let's love up on our spouses the best we can, and hopefully they will love up on us back, you know, so we don't have to divorce their sorry behinds, lol.

7

RE-MARRIAGE

So there you are, happily or sadly single again, having gone through a crazy divorce from someone that you thought was your Mr. or Mrs Right, someone that you thought you were gonna spend the rest of your life with, but, it turned out not to be the case, your marriage ended and now you are free to date anyone you want to, and you are free to fall in love again if you want to, and you are free to get married again if you want to. The question is, why would you want to get married again anyway? I mean, why would you want to put yourself back into an institution that can turn out to be very bad (if things are not working out), why do you want to risk your happiness and or your freedom of being who you really are, or of doing whatever it is you want to do without having to worry about a spouse holding you back? I mean, why would you want to go through having to make all those sacrifices and or compromises that are required in order for a marriage to run smoothly? Have you forgotten already how much work marriages really are? Didn't you say to yourself that you were never doing the marriage thing again after your first marriage ended? Then why are you considering getting married again now, just a few short years after you went through a crazy divorce? Are you that desperate to be with the new person that you are dating, or have you madly fallen in love with the new person you are dating? I think it's both, you are desperate to be with the new person that you are dating because you are madly in love with them, this is the only reason I can see why anyone who has been divorced (especially if their marriage was awful) would want to risk going through another marriage, which could or could not work either. But that's the beauty of falling in love, it makes a person forget (temporarily) the hardship and or unhappiness that they experienced in a previous marriage, and the new love makes them more optimistic that the new person may be the one.

Love is a very powerful thing, it's very hard to fall in love with someone and not want to be with them forever. But as we all know, just because we fall in love with someone it doesn't mean that that is the right person for us, especially when it comes to marriage. So a person who falls in love again with someone new will have to go through the same process of examining their new love interest to see if they are really marriage material or not. And you would think that people who have been married before would be better at examining their new love interest to see if they are marriage material or not, but unfortunately they tend to be just as bad at examining their love interests just as the people who have never been married before. That's why second marriages tend to have the same rate of divorcement as first marriages, and it's because people are just bad at picking marriage partners, whether consciously or subconsciously. And this is because, when people fall in love, they tend to not notice and or to not make a big deal of the flaws that may exist with the people that they are in love with, and this is because they are blinded by love, you know what I mean? And so even people who have been married before can find themselves being blinded by love and end up picking another wrong marriage partner and end up going through another divorce. How disappointing would that be, going through a second divorce, it would be very disappointing, right?

But, that is love, the power of love makes people take chances. And there's no bigger chance taking than getting married, even for the second time. I think people who get married for the second time are brave, because knowing how hard a marriage can be, having already been through it once, they still take the chance to be in another one. I mean, isn't that brave? And think about the people who actually get married three or four times in their lives, wow, how do they do that? I guess there are people who just like being married, and if one marriage doesn't work they just keep on trying. I don't know, I don't think I could do it, get remarried over and over, I think once is all I can do, lol. Maybe it's because I have been married for such a long time that I don't think I would have the strength and or the courage to do it all over again, because even in a marriage that is running smoothly there's still a lot of work that has to go in it to keep it running smoothly, you know what I mean? And of course the work for a couple that has been married a long time won't be as much or as hard as a newly married couple or a couple who has been married for only a few short years, but the work that was put in by the couple that has been married for a long time that enables them to continue to have a smooth marriage is not something that came easily. And this is why you will tend to see people who have been divorced after being in a long time marriage not being in a hurry to get married again, and this is because when they think of all the work that it actually took to make their marriage last for as long as it did, they tend not to be looking forward to putting all that work in again. And this is because it takes a lot of effort to learn how to be married to a spouse, and when you get remarried it will mean you will have to learn how to be married to this new spouse, which could be totally different in how you were used to being in a marriage with the previous spouse, because people are different and what they may require from you will be different. And so you will have to learn how this new spouse likes to do stuff and or how they operate, so that way you can adjust yourself accordingly so the two of you can be in one accord, so that the marriage can run smoothly. All of that adjusting can turn out to be a lot of work, which for a person who has already gone through it with a previous marriage that lasted a long time, they may not want to put themselves through it all over again, you know what I mean?

Experts say that about 4 out of 10 marriages involve a couple in which one partner has been married before, so that means about 40% of all marriages involve a partner who has been divorced before. And out of this 40%, experts say about 20% of it involve couples in which both partners have been married before, which means 20% of all marriages involve couples who have both been divorced before. Wow, that's a lot of divorce and remarriages, isn't it? Experts also say that the divorce rate for second marriages is a little bit higher for second marriages (at about 60%) than for first time marriages (at about 50%). So what does this mean? To me it means that second marriage couples tend to fare less better than first time married couples. And this is interesting, because you would think that couples in second marriages would have learned something about what it really takes to have a successful marriage that they would do better in a second marriage. But it seems like most couples who have been married before don't really learn much from their previous marriages that would help them have a better chance of having a successful second marriage. And I think what happens is, most people who get divorced don't think that they were the problem and or they don't think that they contributed to their marriage not working out. You know, most divorced people think it was the other partner that was the problem, you know, they don't think that they too had something to do with causing the marriage not to work. And so what happens is, one or both partners will bring the same issues that caused their first marriage not to work, they will bring those same issues into their second marriage. They will bring those same issues into their second marriage because they failed to realize that those issues were some of the reasons why their first marriage did not work.

People in relationships are not very good at self reflection, you know, people are not good at examining and accepting that they have some issues that may be detrimental to a relationship. And so these people will take their issues to a new marriage and then get surprised at why their new marriage doesn't seem to be working out either. So it's very important for people who have been married before to take some time and examine themselves first to see if they have some issues that they have not dealt with (help from a professional counselor would be good) that may become an issue in a second marriage before they decide to get married again, because otherwise they may just be setting themselves up for another failed marriage. Because the thing about marriage is, spouses can not hide their true selves to their partners for long, eventually if the partners have any hidden flaws and or issues, those flaws and or issues will end up manifesting themselves sooner than later in the marriage. And what will happen is, those flaws and or issues will start to cause problems in the marriage, if the partners are not well prepared on how to deal with them.

The other reason why second marriages may have a higher rate of divorcement than first marriages is because, the partners in a second marriage may not want to deal with trying to fight for a marriage that they see the signs of not working out, you know, they see the same patterns in their partners that they saw in their previous marriage and they just don't want to go through that whole process of trying to fight for the marriage, because they don't believe there's any chance in it. And what I mean is, the partners in the second marriage tend to want to bail out from their marriages at the first sign of trouble, you know, at the first sign of friction that is starting to present itself in the marriage. And this is because the partners will start to recognize how the problems are starting almost the same way as they did in their previous marriages and they will start to panic, and they will start to think about cutting the marriage short because they don't want to get themselves stuck in a miserable marriage like they were in their first one. And so this is why second marriages tend to have higher divorcement than first marriages, and it's because couples in a first marriage will try to fight as long as they can to keep their marriage, but couples in a second marriage will tend to want to cut their losses early, you know, because they have already been through a miserable marriage before that they fought for but still didn't work out, and so they have no interest in trying to fight that hard for a second marriage that doesn't look like will work out either.

Marriage is a lot of work, and it doesn't matter whether it's first marriage, second, third or fourth marriage, it's all the same, they all require a lot of work to be put into it. And this is because every new person you marry will bring with them their own unique qualities, and you will have to learn how to deal and or handle these unique qualities that each new spouse brings to the new marriage. And so you will have to adjust yourself every time according to the personalities of each spouse that you marry in each marriage, you know, so that way you can be in one accord with each spouse in each marriage that you get into. So remarriage does not guarantee that the second marriage will be better than the first marriage, no, it can even turn out to be worse than the first marriage. And this is how you may sometimes see spouses actually getting back together and remarrying each other, and it's because they divorced each other and went out there in the dating world and realized that the people they were meeting and dating have more issues than they did when they were married, and therefore they realized maybe they should have just stayed together and worked harder on their issues. And then what happens is, they start dating each other again and before long they decide to go ahead and try the marriage thing again with each other, and they remarry each other. Now, of course it's rare that couples that divorce each other end up remarrying each other again, but it does happen.

Love is love, and when a person falls in love the idea of getting married again becomes not as scary, especially if their last previous marriage was not that bad, and or if their previous marriage ended because their spouse died (passed away). There's nothing wrong with getting married again if a person believes they have found a special person who seems to have the potential to make for a good marriage partner. And notice how I said "found a special person", and I said that because there's nothing worse than getting married again and end up in a miserable marriage with a person you knew wasn't even that special, you know, a person you knew was no were close to being marriage material, you know what I mean? And there's no excuse to not knowing what kind of person has the potential of being a good marriage partner if you have been married before, because you should be a lot more wiser in what kind of partner will make for a good union with you by this time, as you should have gained insight and or experience from your previous marriage. So, if you are a person thinking about getting married for the second time, go for it, but just make sure that the person you are considering marrying has real marriage qualities, because you really don't want to end up in another miserable marriage, do you? No, I don't think you do. And I don't want you to end up in another miserable marriage either, because you are too special, and you deserve to be in a good marriage for once, right? Yes you do!!!

8

ARRANGED MARRIAGE

Arranged marriages used to be the most typical way that most marriages were put together back from the ancient times all the way through the modern centuries. It was not until a few centuries ago (2 or 3 centuries ago) that people started choosing whom they wanted to marry. But back in centuries past, sons and daughters who were of marriage age couldn't just go out into the town and choose whom they wanted to marry, no, they had to wait for their families to choose for them whom they would marry. Back in those days marriage was not just a union between the couples, no, in those days marriage was also a union between the two families of the couples. And what I mean is, the two families would be joined together as an alliance through the couples. And this alliance was a real alliance, you know, the two families would actually form a bond and look out for each other. It's like, for example; if a war broke out, those two families would bond together and look out for each other and even fight together against whoever the enemy was. It was a real union between the two families, marriages where strategic moves back in those days. And this is why back in those days Kings and Queens used to be very careful about which kingdoms they would allow their Prince or Princesses to marry into, and it's because they had to make sure they form an alliance with a kingdom that will be strategically beneficial to them and their kingdom both financially and militarily, you know, just in case a war breaks out, they will have a strong kingdom aligned with them to fight whoever the enemy is.

And so what would happen is, families would know way in advance which families they wouldn't mind and or they would like to form an alliance with, and then they would check to see if those families have any sons and or daughters. And then the families would work to get familiar and friendly with those other families that they would like to be aligned with, that way when their children become ready to marry they will already know which families have sons and or daughters and which families they would like their children to marry into. So back in those days marriage wasn't so much about love and or falling in love, no, it was more so about forming a union, not just of the two partners, but also forming a union with other families. But as time went on, sons and daughters started becoming more independent from their families and started becoming more individualized and started falling in love with different kinds of people and started demanding that their families allow them to marry the people that they have fallen in love with, instead of just marrying for strategic family alliances. And this is when marrying for love started becoming more and more popular and or accepted, and it's because sons and daughters started rebelling against their families choosing who they should marry, you know, sons and daughters wanted to have a say on whom they should marry. And so over the centuries and years that followed, marrying for love started becoming more and more popular, and now in our day, it's probably the most popular way of finding a mate, especially in western countries and or westernized countries.

But arranged marriages are still very big in a lot of countries, especially in asian and middle eastern countries, like; India, China, Japan, Pakistan, Iran, Korea, Saudi Arabia, Israel, etc. These countries lead in how many of their marriages are mostly arranged. And it looks like India may be number one in arranged marriages, as it is said that about 95% of all marriages in India are arranged marriages. Wow, that's a huge number, isn't it? And what does this high percentage mean and or indicate? To me, it indicates that there's still some countries where people are not free to love and or fall in love with whomever they want to fall in love with. In these countries, life is still about bringing honor and or forging alliances with other families instead of experiencing individual freedom and or joy of choosing whom to love and whom to be loved by. In these countries bringing honor to the family is everything, and so their sons and daughters are not given the chance to bring dishonor to their families by marrying whomever they want, no, because the chances of the sons and daughters marrying someone that can bring shame to the family is very huge, especially if the families belong to communities that are very strict and or prejudice in matters of like; religion, culture, race, class, education, and so on. And so families do not want to take a chance of having their sons and or daughters falling in love and marrying just anybody, no, because the chances of their sons and or daughters marrying people that not only the family doesn't approve of, but also marrying someone that their communities won't approve of is very high, if the sons and daughters are left to just follow their hearts and marry whomever they want. You know, because the heart can fall in love with anybody, it's all about how that person makes you feel when you are with them, you know what I mean?

And so yeah, arranged marriages are pretty much still very much practiced out here in the world, especially in countries where individual freedom of expression is not valued as much as it does in westernized countries. But nowadays arranged marriages tend not to be as strict as how they used to be back in the day. Because back in the day couples had no idea who they were marrying until the day of the wedding, you know, when the bride would be unveiled and the bride and groom would see each other for the first time ever. It's like, it was almost like a blind date where the two people were set up by their families and they meet for the first time on the date, but in this instance the two people have no choice but to marry the person they first meet in the blind date, no matter whether they are attracted to that person or not, you know what I mean? Can you imagine being set up on a blind date and having to marry the person that you were set up with, even before you had a chance to even talk to them on the blind date. I mean, how awful would that be? I think that would be very awful, especially if you are not attracted to the blind date person at all. But, nowadays the couples tend to kind of know whom they are about to marry, either by pictures and or they may even get to speak to their picked future husbands or wives on the phone before their wedding day. And sometimes nowadays the sons and daughters may even be able to reject whom their families have picked for them, which will mean their families will have to start the search for a suitable spouse for their son or daughter all over again.

So, what do you think about arranged marriages? Do you think they are cruel and unusual punishment for couples, or do you think they are a good tradition for finding marriage partners for couples? Well, I think it depends on how much input the partners have in the arranging process, you know, I think the more the partners are involved, the better the arranged marriage can be, even if the partners don't actually meet each other until the wedding day. And the reason why I say this is because, if the partners have some awareness and or some knowledge about the person whom they are being set up to marry, then they will be more mentally, physically and or emotionally more prepared to be in a marriage with this person. And this is because the partners won't feel like total strangers to each other on their wedding day, because they will be kind of familiar with each other to some extent, even if it's just through seeing pictures of each other and or through talking with each other on the phone.

I also think couples that are being arranged should have the option to reject the person that they are being set up with, at least at the beginning of the process, you know, the beginning before their family goes to talk to the other family about the possibilities of their son or daughter matching up in a marriage together. Because usually after the two families agree to marry their sons and or daughters with each other, there's usually no room for the son or daughter to reject the person that they are being set up with to marry. And this is because when the arrangement process begins, the initial arrangement gifts and or dowry will have started to being exchanged between the families, you know, the groom or the bride's family will have started to give the other family some cows, goats, chickens, money, jewelry and or etc, as part of the dowry. And so what happens is, the family that is receiving these gifts will not want to have to return them if their son or daughter refuses to go through with the wedding. And so the family will make it clear to their son or daughter that they have no option but to get married to the person that the family has chosen for them, otherwise there will be extreme consequences not only to the son or daughter, but also to the family. And some of the consequences can be; the son or daughter can be disowned and or shun by not only their families, but they can be shunned by their communities. And sometimes the daughters can get killed by their own families, because of the dishonor that they have brought to their family by not going through with the wedding. Have you heard of honor killings? Well it's a real thing, especially in these countries that arranged marriages are the norm.

Arranged marriages are serious business in these countries that practice them, because the reputation of the families are strongly involved in it. So sons and daughters pretty much have no choice but to accept whomever their families arrange for them to marry, because they don't want to bring dishonor to their families by being rebellious and refuse to marry the person that their families have chosen for them. And this is also why the divorce rate for arranged marriages is very low (some estimate puts it at around 6 percent world wide), and it's because divorce brings a lot of dishonor not only to the partners, but it brings dishonor also to the families of the partners. And so the couples rarely would even dare try to get divorced, no matter how bad the marriage is, the couples just accept their bad marriages and just learn how to live with it, because the consequences of divorcing can be very severe, to include honor killings. So most couples in arranged marriages are pretty much stuck in their marriages no matter what, even if the marriage involves abuse, both physically and or mentally.

And so there are a lot of disadvantages for arranged marriages, because for one, the partners are pretty much strangers on their wedding day, and for two, if the marriage is bad, there's pretty much no way out of the marriage. And so even though the divorce rate for arranged marriages is very low, it does not mean it's a better method for couples to enter into a marriage, because the uncertainty of the partners being compatible and or the partners being in love with each other can leave the partners with a loveless marriage, which can lead to an unhappy marriage. And also, in an arranged marriage the husband usually has all the authority as head of household, which means whatever he decides goes, no matter if the wife likes it or not. So the women in arranged marriages can easily find themselves not treated as equal partners in their marriages, because they will have no decision making abilities in how their marriage and or their household should be run. So arranged marriages tend to be a little bit harder for the wives than the husbands, because the wives are expected to be very subservient to their husbands, even if their husbands turn out to be idiots and or uncaring.

So, do you think you could handle being in an arranged marriage? Well, I guess it all depends on what kind of spouse you end up with, right? But then again, since you won't have a choice but to learn how to stick to the marriage (since divorce is not really an option), you will have no choice but to learn how to handle being in an arranged marriage, even if you are not really attracted to your arranged spouse. Aren't you glad you were born in a society and or country that does not practice arranged marriage? I know I am! Because I just can't fathom having to marry someone that I may not be even slightly attracted to, you know what I mean? And sure they say that people do grow on you, meaning that you may not be attracted to them at first, but after spending time with them for a long while they can start to be appealing to you, and you can actually start to find them attractive. But I don't know, maybe I'm just too westernized, you know, I just kinda want to find someone attractive at first sight, you know, I want to find someone desirable right off the bat, you know, I want that love at first sight kind of attraction, you know what I mean? But hey, that's life, sometimes we can't choose and or get what we want, sometimes we just have to accept our traditions and just roll with it, you know, even if the tradition seems kinda unfair. So when it comes to arranged marriages, the people who find themselves in those traditions, all they can hope for is that their families love them enough to do their due diligence to find them marriage partners that will be kinda decent, you know, marriage partners that they can at least grow to love and be loved back. Because at the end of the day, that is all that we really want in our marriages, you know, someone who is decent and whom we love and who loves us back. Am I right or what? And I mean, of course we would love to end up with someone who is great and whom we love and who loves us back, but if we can't get someone great, I think we can be ok with someone decent, right? Because truth be told, great people tend to be kinda hard to find, especially nowadays, right?

And so anyway, traditions can be very hard to break, especially if they have been practiced for thousands of years, because the people in these traditions just get so used to them that they feel weird and or uncomfortable changing them. And sometimes societies don't want to change their traditions because it gives them some kind of control over their citizens, especially if freedom of expression and or individualism is not very highly regarded in that society. But, that is life, and that is marriage, we sometimes just have to go with the flow of things and hope that we end up in a good marriage, whether it's arranged or whether we pick it ourselves!

9

POLYGAMY

Polygamy has been around since the beginning of time, it's even in the Bible. Do you know who the first polygamist in the Bible was? It was a guy named Lamech, who was a descendant of Cain (the Cain that killed his brother Abel). Lamech had two wives, and their names were Adah and Zillah. So it looks like polygamy started not long after Adam and Eve started populating the earth. Other notable polygamists in the Bible include; Abraham, who had two wives, and their names were Sarah and Hagar. Some scholars say that Hagar was not a wife but Abraham's concubine. I say what's the difference, they had a child together and lived in the same house with Sarah, that looks like polygamy to me. Am I right or wrong? Another notable Biblical figure that practiced polygamy was Jacob, he was tricked into it though. Because remember how he worked for seven years for the woman he really wanted, the woman he really loved, Rachel. But remember how Rachel's father tricked Jacob by unveiling Rachel's older sister Leah on the wedding day and told Jacob that it was customary for the oldest daughter to be married first before the younger daughter. And then remember how the father told Jacob that if he still wanted to marry Rachel he would have to work seven more years for the father and then he could marry Rachel as well. And remember how poor Jacob had no choice but to agree to work seven more years for Rachel's father so he would be able to marry Rachel. Then after Jacob had finally finished those extra seven years (which makes a total of 14 years that he worked for Rachel's father), he finally was able to marry Rachel, and then left with both Rachel and Leah as his wives. Poor guy, he got tricked into polygamy by the father of the girl he really wanted, and ended up marrying two sisters. And it looks like Jacob had two concubines afterwards, whom he also had children with. Wow, this concubine thing looks like it was an acceptable thing back in those days!

Another notable figure in the Bible that practiced polygamy was King David, he had eight wives. Looks like King David had a little bit of a lusting problem, because remember how he lusted over Bathsheba and then committed adultery with her, and then sent her husband to the front line of a battle so he could get killed so that way King David could take Bathsheba to be his wife. Man, talk about really lusting after a woman, man can do crazy things just to have the woman they lusting after. Another notable figure in the Bible that practiced polygamy is none other than the mack daddy of them all in the Bible, yes you guessed it, it's King Solomon himself. Man, King Solomon was not playing around with this polygamy thing, he went all out with it, you know, he just kept pilling up wives for himself like a kid in a candy store. I mean, King Solomon was a big time player from the himalayas when it came to women, he's lust for women surpassed his father King David. He made King David's 8 wives look like a very small number, because King Solomon had 700 wives, yes you read that right, the Bible says he had 700 wives. How the heck does someone have 700 wives? I mean, I know how you can get to 700 wives, you just keep getting married, over and over and over and over and over again, you know, till you get to 700. I mean, isn't that crazy, all those wives!? But, it gets even crazier, as, not only did King Solomon have 700 wives, he also had 300 concubines! What, why would anybody need concubines when they already have 700 wives, how greedy is that?! Man, isn't that wild? And how was King Solomon able to handle and or satisfy all those women? Because the total of all those women is one thousand (1,000). How the heck does a man satisfy 1,000 women on a regular basis? It's impossible, because there are only 365 days a year, so there's no way King Solomon was able to satisfy all those women on a regular basis, heck there's no way he was able to see all those women on a regular basis, you know what I mean? I mean, even if he spent per day with two of his women at a time, he would run out of days in the calendar year to spend time with all of his 1,000 women. The only way he would have been able to spend time with all of his women in one year is if he spent time with 3 of his women per day, every day for the whole year. How crazy would that be? He must have been exhausted all the time, unless they had some super energy drinks back in those days, you know what I mean, lol!

And so anyway, yeah, polygamy has been around since the Bible days, but it started not being as common as the centuries went on up to today, in our time. Nowadays polygamy is not as common a practice in most of society, but there's still parts of the world where it is still strongly practiced. Polygamy is legal in most countries in Africa, but it is more strongly practiced in West and Central Africa, with Nigeria, Mali, Senegal and Burkina Faso leading the way. Polygamy is illegal in all European countries, but Sweden and Switzerland will recognize a polygamous marriage that was performed in another country were it is legal. Polygamy is legal in most countries in the Middle East, but the practice doesn't seem to be that widespread. In India, Malaysia, the Philippines and Singapore, polygamy is legal only for Muslims. Polygamy is illegal in Russia, China and almost all Asian countries. Polygamy is illegal in Australia, North America (United States and Canada) and South America. I think I have covered the whole world showing that polygamy is not that widely practiced anymore. But there are places where they still practice, like West Africa, where having two or three wives is kind of a normal thing. And countries that have majority and or a large segment of their population are Muslims, the practice of polygamy tends to be more common. And this is because Muslims are actually allowed to have more than one wife according to their holy book the Koran, which actually encourages them to marry many wives up to four. And the reason for this allowance they say is because since there are a lot more women in the world than men, then if men only marry one wife, that will mean there will be a lot of women who won't get a chance to be married and have their own families, you know, they won't have a chance to have children and a husband. They won't have a chance to have children because they won't have a husband to get them pregnant, because women were only supposed to bring forth children after they were married, you know what I mean?

So yeah, polygamy is not that widespread anymore but there's still places where it's being practiced. And even in the United States there a few clusters of folks practicing polygamy, especially in Utah, largely in the Mormon community. Not all mormons practice polygamy, but there are clusters who broke off from the main Mormon Church of

Later-day Saints. These clusters refuse to give up polygamy, as they claim it's part of their religion. And Utah just decriminalized polygamy not that long ago, making it a small infraction were the practitioners can just pay a small fine if caught. So, if you thinking of practicing polygamy my friends out there who are reading this, Utah may be the place to go practice at, you know, so you can live happily like a king, with your 700 wives like King Solomon, you know what I mean, fellas, lol!

I think polygamy is a fantasy that almost every man has, you know, to have a bunch of wives, not just two, more like three or four, lol! Am I right or what, fellas!? I mean, wouldn't that be the dream, you know, when you get tired of dealing with one wife you go chill with the next wife, and when you get tired dealing with her you go chill with wife number 3, and if wife number 3 has an attitude you got chill with wife number 4, you know what I mean fellas!? How great would that be fellas, wouldn't that be fantastic? Sorry ladies, I'm just talking to the fellas here for a few seconds, a few sentences of pow wow time with the guys, you know, the men cave section of the book, no ladies allowed in these sentences until the next paragraph, is that alright with you ladies? No, it's not alright, us guys can't have a private section (just one paragraph) in the book for our men cave discussions? Oh wow, even in a book us men can't have our private men time to discuss our multiple wives fantasies, smh! Okay fine ladies, let me ask you a question then, would you let your husband marry a second wife so you can have a sister wife who can help you with taking care of the house and raising the children? No, why not? Oh, let me guess, you don't want to share your husband with no other woman hah? Okay fine, but don't bother us men when we trying to watch our sports in peace, you could have had a sister wife to help you with whatever you need help with during the times we men are watching our sports, but you refused a sister wife, so don't bother us please during our sports time, okay, thank you! Hey fellas, I tried to get you a second wife but the ladies nowadays are not going for it, I don't really understand why they don't see the benefit of a sister wife, but hey, it's their loss, lol!

Hey, hey, hey ladies, I'm just playing, just joking around, no need to get all defensive, talking to yourself saying "who does this author think he is, trying to tell us to share our husband with a sister wife"!? I bet you that's what you were thinking ladies as you read the above paragraph. Email me and let me know if I'm wrong, lol. Anyway, no one wants to marry more than one wife, not us westernized men, oh no, we have enough trouble trying to deal with just one wife, one westernized wife is enough for us, lol! I can just imagine trying to deal with 4 westernized wives, oh boy, all I can see is multiple headaches, quadruple headaches, lol. And why do I say this, it's because westernized wives have no problem confronting their husbands with whatever they don't like that the husband has done or not done. And so imagine 4 westernized wives confronting their shared husband, oh boy, quadruple headaches, lol. So ladies, be rest assured we westernized men don't want no multiple wives, no, we just want one sexy westernized wife to drive us crazy, not two, or three, or four, no, just one wonderful wife will do.

Polygamy is a very interesting marriage concept, and it has it's advantages and disadvantages, especially for women in economically challenged countries.   The reason I say this is because, in economically challenged countries, it's very hard for a lot of women to be financially independent. You know, it's very hard for a lot of women to be able to take care of themselves financially. And this is because employment opportunities in these countries are very limited and hard to find. And since women are usually marginalized in these countries, any employment opportunity will first go to the men, which leaves a lot of women jobless and having to find another way to hustle so they can sustain themselves financially, which can be very challenging. And so, having a husband for these women tends to be a better option for them, even if they end up being a second, third, or fourth wife, because since husbands are supposed to look after all their wives, the women know that they will gain some financial and or material assistance that will help make their lives a little bit more stable.

I remember when I went back home (Tanzania) for a visit, I remember talking to one of my female cousins about life and relationships, and I remember her telling me that she was dating a guy, but the guy's ex-girlfriend decided to come back to the guy not long after my cousin started dating him.   And what happened was, the guy used to try to get his ex-girlfriend to come back to him but she kept refusing because he wouldn't propose marriage to her, so she felt like he was wasting her time, so she left him. So not long after, the guy moved on and started dating my cousin. But word soon got back to his ex and her family about him dating another woman. When her family heard that, they told her to hurry up and go back to the guy and they will make sure that the guy proposes marriage to her. And the reason why they told her to hurry and go back to the guy is because they didn't want another woman taking her spot as a potential wife to the guy, because the guy was kinda well off, you know, the guy had money.

So what happened was, my cousin told me that the guy called her one day and told her that his ex-girlfriend came back to him, but he is not sure what to do, because he really likes my cousin but he is getting family pressure to stay with his ex and to marry her. Apparently what happened was, his ex's family went to speak with the guy's family and told them that it is shameful what their son is doing to their daughter, because he has lived with her for almost 5 years and hasn't married her yet, and that's why she had left him. They also said that living together for almost 5 years pretty much makes them common law husband and wife, and so it would be the right thing to do for their son (the guy) to go ahead and marry their daughter, to remove the shame. And it looks like the guy's family agreed with the ex-girlfriend's family, because the guy told my cousin that he is getting pressure to marry his ex-girlfriend from his own family. So my cousin told me that she told him that if he is getting pressure from his own family, then it may be a good idea for him to go ahead and marry his ex-girlfriend, because if he doesn't marry his ex-girlfriend (whom his family has known for almost five years) and then wants to marry my cousin, it not only will look like my cousin was the cause for him not to marry who his family preferred for him to marry, but my cousin will most likely end up having a very awkward and or bad relationship with his family, because his family may not totally accept her. And my cousin told me that she told him that maybe later down the road she can be his second wife, but she will think about it.

I remember sitting there on the couch looking at her to see if she was serious or not about considering being a second wife. But she was serious! I remember telling her that she is first wife material, not second wife material. She told me she knows she is first wife material, but, if the guy marries his ex, then she would be ok being his second wife, because she knows the guy will take care of her, you know, he will look out for her financially. She said plus, it will probably be easier to be a second wife than a first wife. And her reasoning was because, much more tends to be expected from first wives than from second wives (especially if they live in different households, were the second wife has her own place), and as a second wife that means she won't have to deal with the guy everyday, a few days a week would be just fine for her, that's what she said. She said men can be real trifling, they can start out all sweet, but then after they marry you they can become trifling. And she said she doesn't have the energy to deal with a trifling husband everyday of the week, twice a week that she can do with no problem, because she'll know she will have the rest of the week to herself for some peace. I laughed, and then asked her, what if he wants children!? She said that's fine, she can give him one child, and he can come over for two days a week, and then go back to his first wife. She had me laughing, but she was serious! You see, my cousin has been married before but the marriage wasn't good, she is now divorced and not really looking to get married again anytime soon, unless it's as a second wife to the guy she's dating, because he's got money.

And so you see, that's one of the advantages of being in a polygamous marriage, a woman gets a chance to not only have a husband (husbands can be hard to find sometimes, especially in economically challenged countries), but she gets a chance to be assisted financially, even if she's a second or third or fourth wife, because husbands are supposed to take care of all their wives. Also, in a lot of these countries an unmarried woman can really be looked down upon, especially if she's in her late twenties and over, and has never been married before. And so attaching herself to a husband can bring her some kind of esteem in the community, even if she's a second, third, or fourth wife, especially if she is married to a man that has money and or is well respected in the community.

Polygamy even though it can have some advantages, it does have some disadvantages as well. And the biggest disadvantage is, the wives have to share one husband, which means the wives don't truly get the experience of being totally loved every day by their husband, because their husband has to divide his time and love between the wives. And so, polygamy actually cheats wives a chance of receiving 100% of love and attention from their husbands, as their husbands attention has to be split among the wives. Polygamy can leave the wives feeling not loved enough, not cared enough, and or not wanted enough by their husbands, as they have to wait for their turn to be with him, especially if all the wives live in separate households. Polygamy is actually not an easy life style, because it requires for the wives to be extra selfless in the marriage, because their husband doesn't belong to just them, he belongs to two, three or four other women who are also his wives. I don't know, I couldn't do it, I'm not that selfless, I just couldn't handle seeing my lover being romantic with other people, no, sorry, I couldn't do it. But if you are in a polygamous marriage you have to be able to do it, you know, you have to be able to handle knowing that your lover is making love to other people, not just you. I don't know, it takes a whole different kind of mindset for a person to be ok with their lover making love to other people, instead of just them. And not just making love to other people from time to time, no, making love to other people all the time on a regular basis, you know what I mean? I don't know, I couldn't do it, I'm just too selfish when it comes to my lover, I don't want anybody else to make love to my lover besides me, no, stay away from my lover, she's mine, and mine alone lol!

But hey, that's polygamy for you, sharing a lover, aka sharing a husband. What do you think, could you do it, would you be ok with sharing your lover with someone else? Let's say there was a shortage of men out there (ladies), and the only way to have a man in your life would be to share him with another woman, would you do it, would you share a man with another woman? You are probably shaking your head right now side to side indicating "NO" way, big fat no. Are you sure? Are you sure you wouldn't want to feel the embrace of a lover (man), even if you have to share him with another woman? No, nope, never!? Yeah right, you're just saying that because you know you have options. Because we who have options have a hard time understanding how anyone would want to be in a relationship with someone who is seeing other people and they are ok about it, you know what I mean? But there's women out there who don't think and or don't feel like they have options (whether true or not), because there's places where there's a whole lot more women than men, therefore the women feel like they have no option but to marry a man who already has one, two, or three other wives. But hey, we can't really judge anyone who finds themselves in a polygamous marriage, they have their own reasons, all we can hope for is they find some kind of joy and or happiness in the marriage lifestyle that they have chosen or that has chosen them!

10

HAPPILY EVER AFTER

How wonderful would it be to find that one person on a planet of billions of people that truly understands you and truly cares for you? Wouldn't that be so wonderful? Yes it would be! And how wonderful would it be to fall in love with someone who has also fallen in love with you and the two of you end up getting married to each other? Wouldn't that be so wonderful? Yes it would be! And how wonderful would it be to be married to someone who is not just your husband or wife but they are also your best friend? Wouldn't that be so wonderful? Yes it would be! And how wonderful would it be to be married to someone who truly appreciates you and whom you truly appreciate, and the two of you live happily ever after, until both of you are old and gray? Wouldn't that be so wonderful? Yes it would be!

The dream and hope of every newlywed couple is that they live happily ever after with their spouse. They hope that their marriage will last forever, you know, they hope to grow old together, until death do them part. Wouldn't that be lovely, to be married to your spouse for 20, 30, 40, 50, 60, 70 years. I mean, how lovely would that be!? I think that would be fantastic, especially if the marriage is a good one. Can you imagine being married to the same person for 60 or 70 years? Wow, that has to be a very wonderful experience! And this is what every newlywed hopes for, to spend the rest of their lives with the person they fell in love with. But, as we all know, not many marriages get to happily ever after. And this is because marriage is hard work, both partners have to be truly committed to the marriage for it to have a chance at getting to happily ever after. Can you imagine how much work the couple that actually makes it to happily ever after must have put in for them to be married that long, 30, 40, 50, 60, years of marriage. That is awesome stuff! And I admire couples who have been married that long, because I know they had to put in some work into their marriage for it to last that long. Because the thing is, as people grow older, they tend to change a little bit as they age. You know, the person you married when the two of you were in your twenties won't be the same exact person (physically, mentally, spiritually, etc) you will still be married to when you are in your 40s, 50s, or 60s. And what I mean is, for example; a spouse's outlook on life can change as they get older, or a spouse's spirituality can change as they get older, or a spouse can have health issues, or a spouse can be disabled, or etc. So there's some personal changes that spouses will have to deal with as they get older, and their partners will have to learn how to deal with them as they change. For example: say you married someone who was an optimist, but as life went on they became pessimist. What are you going to do? You are not going to divorce them because now they are all gloom and doom, are you? No, you are now going to learn how to be married to a pessimist. Another example can be; you married someone who was very religious, you know, was deep into going to church and all those kinds of things, but as time went on they became less religious, not interested in going to church that much, if at all. What are you going to do? You are not going to divorce them because now they are less religious, are you?

There are many other examples I'm sure you can think of in how spouses can change from how they were when you first married them to how they are now, 10, 20, 30 years later. So this is what I mean by saying that who you marry today won't be the same exact person you will still be married to years later down the road, and it's because as people grow older their outlook on life and other things about them can change, to some degree. So for a couple to be able to maintain their marriage for the long haul, they will have to learn how to deal with their spouses in whatever way their spouses may change. And this is why I admire couples who have been married for such a long time, and it's because it shows that they were able to adjust to how each spouse may have changed overtime. And so for a marriage to have a chance at getting to happily ever after, the two partners have to really be committed to the marriage and learn how to be married to each other no matter the personal changes that each partner may go through.

When I was younger (before I got married), I used to say to myself that if I ever get married I hope I will be one of those people that will have been married for a very long time to the same wife. And the reason for it is because, for one; I always thought it was so cute to see those old couples that have been married like forever to each other, and they walking around still holding hands and looking at each other so lovingly. And for two; I always said to myself that if I ever get married I'm only going to do it one time, you know, I'm only going to do the marriage thing one time and if it doesn't work out I'm never getting married again. And this is because I had already sensed that marriage is not an easy institution, just from observing my surroundings of how many marriages didn't work out and the couples had to divorce. That told me and or informed me that this marriage institution thing must not be an easy thing, but I always knew that I wanted to try it at least once, that's it, one and done. But I thank God that so far so good, you know, so far me and my wife seem to still be in one accord, you know, me and my wife seem to still like and love each other. And did you notice how I said "like", and the reason I said that is because it is possible for couples to still love each other but not like each other, do you know what I mean? What I mean is, to love someone means to truly care about them, so it is possible to truly care about someone but not to like them. I mean it's like, you may really care about your partner and not want anything bad and or hurt to happen to them, but you may not like your partner because they keep doing things that upset you and or get on your nerves, so even though you truly love them, you may not like them that much or not like them at all anymore. It's very important to like your partner and for your partner to like you, because "like" is what will make the two of you to still want to be together, because the both of you will still enjoy being around each other. And that's it, that's the secret to a long marriage, and it's to still like each other and not to get in each other's nerves too much all the time, because it can get tiring after a while to where one or both of you will start to hate being around each other, you know what I mean?

Marriage can be a challenge to maintain for the long haul, but if you have the right partner, the possibilities are there for the two of you to make it to the end. It really comes down to how well you and your partner match up, you know, how well the two of you get along. How well the two of you match up will determine how well the two of you will get along in the marriage. And by matching I mean character wise, you know, like temperament, demeanor, outlook on life, etc. It's also about how the two of you care for each other, you know, how the two of you look out for each other. And so if you marry a partner who's temperament compliments your temperament, you will have a good chance of having a long marriage, because the two of you will have a good understanding of each other, because your temperaments will be kind of similar. So if you marry a partner who matches up with you well, your marriage won't be too much of a challenge, because the two of you will have a very good understanding of each other, which will make the marriage run smoothly, even if a few frictions pop up here and there. And this is why I admire couples who have been married for a long time, and it's because it shows that they have learned how to deal and or resolve those little frictions that tend to pop up here and there in a marriage. And that's really it, that's really the secret to having a long marriage, and it's the couple learning how to deal and or resolve those little frictions and or issues that tend to pop up here and there in their marriage.

Marriage, it can be the most wonderful institution if it's working, but it can be the most awful institution if it's not working. Am I right or wrong? I believe I am right! So be careful on whom you decide to make your marriage partner, because if they don't match well with you, you can easily find yourself trapped in a miserable marriage, and who wants that, not me, not you, not nobody, right!? We all want to be married happily ever after to the people we fall in love with, that's why we got married to them in the first place, right? Yes, that's right! So couples, take care of each other out there, wives take care of your husbands and husbands take care of your wives, because there's nothing more wonderful than seeing an old couple all lovie dovie over each other, as they live happily ever after!

Well my friends, that's it, that's all I have to say about marriage, hopefully you enjoyed reading the book as much as I enjoyed writing it. I hope the book was informative, entertaining, and inspiring, because that was the aim. So hey you lovers, go out there and find your Mr. or Mrs. Right, and when you do, marry them, cherish them, love them, and enjoy them, because there's nothing more joyous in the world than going through this journey of life with the person that you are in love with. I wish you much love, peace, and happiness, Dear Reader, yes you, be blessed, I'm out!!!